YOUR P[illegible]L

SCORPIO

Your Personal Horoscope 2010

♏

Scorpio

24th October–22nd November

igloo

igloo

This edition published by Igloo Books Ltd,
Cottage Farm, Sywell, Northants NN6 0BJ
www.igloo-books.com

Produced for Igloo Books by W. Foulsham & Co. Ltd,
The Oriel, Thames Valley Court, 183–187 Bath Road, Slough,
Berkshire SL1 4AA, England

ISBN: 978-1-84817-694-2

This is an abridged version of material originally published in *Old Moore's Horoscope and Astral Diary*.

Printed and manufactured in China

CONTENTS

INTRODUCTION

Your Personal Horoscopes have been specifically created to allow you to get the most from astrological patterns and the way they have a bearing on not only your zodiac sign, but nuances within it. Using the diary section of the book you can read about the influences and possibilities of each and every day of the year. It will be possible for you to see when you are likely to be cheerful and happy or those times when your nature is in retreat and you will be more circumspect. The diary will help to give you a feel for the specific 'cycles' of astrology and the way they can subtly change your day-to-day life. For example, when you see the sign ☿, this means that the planet Mercury is retrograde at that time. Retrograde means it appears to be running backwards through the zodiac. Such a happening has a significant effect on communication skills, but this is only one small aspect of how the Personal Horoscope can help you.

With Your Personal Horoscope the story doesn't end with the diary pages. It includes simple ways for you to work out the zodiac sign the Moon occupied at the time of your birth, and what this means for your personality. In addition, if you know the time of day you were born, it is possible to discover your Ascendant, yet another important guide to your personal make-up and potential.

Many readers are interested in relationships and in knowing how well they get on with people of other astrological signs. You might also be interested in the way you appear to very different sorts of individuals. If you are such a person, the section on Venus will be of particular interest. Despite the rapidly changing position of this planet, you can work out your Venus sign, and learn what bearing it will have on your life.

Using Your Personal Horoscope you can travel on one of the most fascinating and rewarding journeys that anyone can take – the journey to a better realisation of self.

THE ESSENCE OF SCORPIO

Exploring the Personality of Scorpio the Scorpion

(24TH OCTOBER – 22ND NOVEMBER)

What's in a sign?

To say that you are a little complicated and somewhat difficult to understand is probably a great understatement. The basic reason for this lies in the peculiar nature of Scorpio rulership. In terms of the elements, your zodiac sign is a Water sign. This makes you naturally emotional, deep, somewhat reserved and ever anxious to help those around you. As a direct contrast, classical astrologers always maintained that your planetary ruler was Mars. Mars is the planet of combat and aggression, being positive and dominant under most circumstances. So it can be judged from the start that there are great contradictions within the basic Scorpio nature.

It's a fact that many people are naturally cautious of Scorpio people. Perhaps this isn't surprising. Under most circumstances you appear to be quiet and peaceful, but the situation is a little like a smoking bomb. When it comes to defending yourself, or in particular those people who you see as being important to you, there is virtually no limit to which you would refuse to go. Generally speaking our ancient ancestors were extremely wise in terms of the names they gave to the different zodiac signs. Consider the apparently diminutive and retiring scorpion. It doesn't go looking for trouble and is generally happy to remain in the shadows. However, if it is provoked, or even attacked, it will take on adversaries many times its own size. It carries a barbed sting in its tail and will strike without any additional warning if necessary.

All the same, the Scorpio reputation may be a little undeserved. Yours is one of the most compassionate and caring of all the zodiac signs. When it comes to working on behalf of humanity, especially the oppressed, the sick or the disenfranchised, you show your true mettle. You cannot stand the thought of people suffering unjustifiably, which is why many of the great social reformers and even freedom fighters had the same zodiac sign as you do.

As a Scorpio you are likely to be intuitive (some would say psychic) and under most circumstances you are more than willing to follow that little voice inside yourself that tells you how to behave in any given situation.

Scorpio resources

Your nature is so very often understated that it might be said that your greatest resource is surprise. You have the ability to shock people constantly, even those who think they understand you perfectly well. This brings us back to the creature for which your zodiac sign is named. A scorpion is diminutive – and would represent a tasty snack for any would-be predator. However, it defies logic by standing its ground and fighting back. When it does, woe betide the aggressor that refuses to take account of its presence. And so it is with you. Quiet, even reserved, you tend to get on with your work. This you do efficiently and without undue fuss, approaching each task with the same methodical attitude. People often don't even realise that you are around. And then, when they least expect it, there you are!

The ability to surprise means that you often get on in life against heavy odds. In addition you have great resilience and fortitude. It is possible for you to continue to work long and hard under circumstances that would force others to retreat. Most Scorpio people would not consider themselves to be tough – in fact quite a few are positively neurotic when it comes to matters associated with their own health. Yet you can endure hardship well and almost always win through in the end.

It's true that you may not be quite as confident as you could be. If you were, people would notice you more and that would detract from that all-important element of surprise that makes you so formidable, and which is definitely the most important weapon in your armoury. However, it is clear that your greatest resource is compassion, and on those occasions when you really allow it to show, you display yourself as being one of the most important allies to your fellow men and women.

At a practical level you are more than capable and can often be expected to perform tasks that you haven't necessarily undertaken before. You have a deep intelligence and good powers to reason things out. Most important of all is a determination that no other zodiac sign can match.

Beneath the surface

This section of an account of the typical Scorpio nature could fill an entire book in itself because you are such a complicated person. However, there are certain advantages to being a Scorpio. For example, nobody is going to run away with the idea that you are basically uncomplicated and shallow. It ought to be clear enough to the dullest observer that there is a boiling, seething volcano bubbling away beneath the surface of almost every Scorpio subject.

You are often accused of having a slightly dark view of life, and it's true that many Scorpio people enjoy a rather morbid curiosity and are fascinated by subjects that make other people shudder. At the same time you could hardly be described as being one of life's natural optimists. Part of the reason for this lies in the fact that you have been disappointed in the past and may have arrived at the conclusion that to expect the worst is often the most sensible course of action. At least that way you are likely to mitigate some of the potential depression regarding failures in the future.

Although this way of thinking is somewhat faulty, it comes so naturally to the Scorpio subject that it actually works very well, though it has to be said that it might be responsible for a tendency to hold back on occasions.

Assessing the way your inner mind works is as difficult for you as it is for any outsider. Even individuals who have been friends for years will sometimes come desperately unstuck if they arrive at the conclusion that they know well what makes you tick. In the recesses of your mind you are passionate, driving, restless, dissatisfied and frequently disappointed with your own efforts. On the other hand, you have the power to make dreams into realities and are excellent at hatching plans that will benefit people far from your own circle and circumstances. Being a tireless worker on behalf of the oppressed, the fate of humanity as a whole is ever an inner concern.

When you love you do so with great width and depth. Your capacity for jealousy knows no bounds and there are times when you can be as destructive to yourself as you ever could be regarding any other individual. Yet for all this your inner mind is lofty and can soar like an eagle on occasions. If the world at large was able to fathom just one tenth of the way your inner mind actually works, people would find you even more fascinating than they do already. But perhaps it's best that they don't. The deepest recesses of Scorpio are an intense secret and will usually stay that way.

Making the best of yourself

It isn't hard to find a single word that describes the way you can make the best of yourself, especially when viewed by the world at large. That word is 'communication'. When difficulties arise in your life, especially concerning other people, it's usually because you haven't managed to get your message across, and probably because you haven't even tried to do so. There is much to your nature that is electric, powerful and magnetic. These qualities make you potentially popular and fascinating to a wealth of individuals. Hide these qualities beneath too brusque an exterior and you can seem dark and brooding.

Of course it's a fine line and one that isn't easy to walk. You are constantly worried that if you show people what really makes you tick, they will not find you interesting at all. In reality this concern is totally without foundation. There is more than enough depth about you to last several lifetimes. It doesn't matter how much you give of yourself to the world at large, there are always going to be surprises galore to follow.

Use the dynamic qualities of your nature to the full. Traditionally your ruling planet is Mars – a real go-getter of a planetary ruler and one that imbues you with tremendous power to get things done at a practical level. On the way you need to show how much you care about others. Amidst a plethora of gifts offered to you by the celestial spheres, your ability to help others is likely to be top of the list. When you are giving you are also usually approachable. For you the two go hand in hand. Avoid allowing yourself to become morose or inward looking and always strive to find simple answers to simple questions.

Stick to some sort of work that you find interesting. That can be almost anything to a Scorpio, as long as it feeds the inner you. It does need to carry a degree of diversity and should ideally have an end product that is easy to see. On your journey through life don't get carried away with daydreams – yet on the other hand avoid losing your great potential to make them come true.

The impressions you give

This is one area of your life over which you do have a great deal of control. If the adage 'what you see is what you get' turns out to be true for many signs of the zodiac, it certainly isn't the case with you. The complexity of your nature makes it difficult for even you to find 'the real Scorpio', and in any case this tends to change from day to day. However, regarding some matters there isn't any doubt at all. Firstly you are deeply magnetic and possess the ability to arouse an instinctive fascination in others. Ally this to your propensity for being very positive in your decision making and you have a potentially formidable combination.

Most people already think of you as being an extremely interesting person. Unfortunately they may also occasionally consider you to be a little cool and somewhat difficult to approach. Neither of these impressions are true, it's simply that you are quite shy at heart, and sometimes find it difficult to believe that you could be liked by certain individuals. Learn to throw this erroneous assumption out of the window, and instead, expect to be viewed positively. To do so would make all the difference and would clear the way so that your more personable side can show all the time.

Very few people who know you well could fail to realise that you care deeply, especially about the well-being of the oppressed. You have a truly noble spirit, a fact that shines through in practically everything you do – yet another reason to be noticed.

It's true that you can sometimes make your secretive quality into an art form, which those looking in from the outside might find rather difficult to deal with. This represents another outward aspect of your nature that could so easily be altered. By all means keep your secrets, though not about matters that are of no real note whatsoever. In a single phrase, try to lighten up a little. It's all you need to be almost perfect!

The way forward

It must first be held in mind that Scorpio people are complicated. That's something you simply cannot get away from, no matter how much you might try. On the one hand you can deal with practical matters almost instinctively. You are resourceful, deep thinking, intense and fascinating. On the other side of the coin you are often too fond of luxury and will frequently withdraw yourself from situations that you do not care to pursue. You can be quite stubborn and can even bear a grudge if you feel that you have been provoked. It is suggested in astrology that no quality of nature is necessarily good or bad, it really depends on the way it is used. For example, stubbornness can be considered a terrible fault, but not if you were being awkward concerning the obvious rights of an oppressed person or group. It turns out that Scorpio has more of a potential to be 'saint or sinner' than any zodiac sign. As long as you examine your motives in any given situation, whilst at the same time trying to cultivate a degree of flexibility that is not one of your natural gifts, then you won't go far wrong.

Turn on the charm when it is necessary because it will rarely if ever let you down. Think about the way you can serve the world, but don't preach about it. Love sincerely, but don't allow jealousy to spoil things. Be constructive in your determination and don't get on your high horse when it isn't necessary. Follow these simple rules for the best chance of progress.

Of course there are many positives around to start with. You are a very loyal friend, are capable of being extremely brave and tend to be very committed to family members. At the same time you are trustworthy and can work long and hard using your own initiative. Although you sometimes worry about your health, you are more robust than most and can endure a high degree of hardship if necessary. You don't take kindly to criticism but can be flexible enough to accept it if you know it is intended for your own good.

Few people doubt your sincerity – that is, when they know what you believe. So it's important to lay your thoughts on the line right from the start. And even if you don't choose to treat the whole world as a friend, you are capable of gathering a little circle around you who would never let you down. Do make sure, however, that this 'inner group' isn't simply comprised of other Scorpios!

SCORPIO ON THE CUSP

Astrological profiles are altered for those people born at either the beginning or the end of a zodiac sign, or, more properly, on the cusps of a sign. In the case of Scorpio this would be on the 24th of October and for two or three days after, and similarly at the end of the sign, probably from the 20th to the 22nd of November.

The Libra Cusp – October 24th to 26th

You are probably generally considered to be a bright and breezy sort of character, with a great deal of enthusiasm for life. Despite this, few people would doubt that you are a shrewd operator, and that you know what you want and have a fairly good idea of how to go about getting it. Not everyone likes you as much as you would wish, but that's because the Libran side of your nature longs for popularity, while set against this is your deep Scorpio need to speak your mind, even when you know that other people might wish you did not indulge in this trait very frequently.

In love, you typify the split between these two signs. On the one hand you are passionate, sincere and intense, while on the other your Libran responses can cause a certain fickle sort of affection to show sometimes, probably to the confusion of those with whom you are involved at a personal level. Nevertheless, few people would find fault with your basic nature and there isn't much doubt that your heart is in the right place.

When it comes to career matters, you have a very fortunate combination. Scorpio can sometimes be accused of lacking diplomacy, but nothing could be further from the truth with Libra. As a result, you have what it takes in terms of determination but at the same time you are capable of seeing the point of view put forward by colleagues. You tend to rise to the top of the tree and, with your mixture of raw ability and humour that most of the world approves of, you can stay there.

You won't be the sort of person to make quite as many enemies as Scorpio taken alone might do, and you need the cut and thrust of the world much more than the retiring creature after whom your zodiac sign is named. Try not to be controversial and do your best to retain a sense of humour, which is essential to your well-being. Few would doubt the fact that your heart is in the right place and your creative potential could be second to none. Most important of all, you need the self-satisfaction that comes from living in the real world.

The Sagittarius Cusp – November 20th to 22nd

You can be a really zany character, with a love of life that is second to none. Add to this a penetrating insight, a razor-sharp wit and an instinctive intuition that is quite remarkable and we find in you a formidable person. It's true that not everyone understands what makes you tick, probably least of all yourself, but you strive to be liked and really do want to advertise your willingness to learn and to grow, which isn't always the province of Scorpio when taken alone. Your capacity for work knows no bounds, though you don't really like to get your hands dirty and would feel more content when telling others what to do.

In a career sense, you need to be in a position from which you are able to delegate. This is not because you are afraid of hard work yourself, far from it, but you possess a strong ability to see through problems and you are a natural director of others. Sales careers may interest you, or a position from which you can organise and arrange things. However, you hate to be tied down to one place for long, so you would be at your best when allowed to move around freely and do things in your own way.

You are a natural social reformer, mainly because you are sure that you know what is right and just. In the main you are correct in your assumptions, but there are occasions when you should realise that there is more than one form of truth. Perhaps you are not always quite as patient with certain individuals as you might be but these generally tend to be people who show traits of cruelty or cunning. As a family person, you care very much for the people who figure most prominently in your life. Sometimes you are a definite home bird, with a preference for what you know and love, but this is offset by a restless trend within your nature that often sends you off into the wide blue yonder, chasing rainbows that the Scorpio side of your nature doubts are even there. Few would doubt your charm, your magnetism, or your desire to get ahead in life in almost any way possible. You combine patience with genuine talent and make a loyal, interesting and entertaining friend or lover.

SCORPIO AND ITS ASCENDANTS

The nature of every individual on the planet is composed of the rich variety of zodiac signs and planetary positions that were present at the time of their birth. Your Sun sign, which in your case is Scorpio, is one of the many factors when it comes to assessing the unique person you are. Probably the most important consideration, other than your Sun sign, is to establish the zodiac sign that was rising over the eastern horizon at the time that you were born. This is your Ascending or Rising sign. Most popular astrology fails to take account of the Ascendant, and yet its importance remains with you from the very moment of your birth, through every day of your life. The Ascendant is evident in the way you approach the world, and so, when meeting a person for the first time, it is this astrological influence that you are most likely to notice first. Our Ascending sign essentially represents what we appear to be, while the Sun sign is what we feel inside ourselves.

The Ascendant also has the potential for modifying our overall nature. For example, if you were born at a time of day when Scorpio was passing over the eastern horizon (this would be around the time of dawn) then you would be classed as a double Scorpio. As such, you would typify this zodiac sign, both internally and in your dealings with others. However, if your Ascendant sign turned out to be a Fire sign, such as Aries, there would be a profound alteration of nature, away from the expected qualities of Scorpio.

One of the reasons why popular astrology often ignores the Ascendant is that it has always been rather difficult to establish. We have found a way to make this possible by devising an easy-to-use table, which you will find on page 157 of this book. Using this, you can establish your Ascendant sign at a glance. You will need to know your rough time of birth, then it is simply a case of following the instructions.

For those readers who have no idea of their time of birth it might be worth allowing a good friend, or perhaps your partner, to read through the section that follows this introduction. Someone who deals with you on a regular basis may easily discover your Ascending sign, even though you could have some difficulty establishing it for yourself. A good understanding of this component of your nature is essential if you want to be aware of that 'other person' who is responsible for the way you make contact with the world at large. Your Sun sign, Ascendant sign, and the other pointers in this book will, together, allow you a far better understanding of what makes you tick as an individual. Peeling back the different layers of your astrological make-up can be an enlightening experience, and the Ascendant may represent one of the most important layers of all.

Scorpio with Scorpio Ascendant

This is one of the most potent of all astrological possibilities, but how it is used depends so very much on the individual who possesses it. On the one hand you are magnetic, alluring, sexy, deep and very attractive, whilst at the same time you are capable of being stubborn, self-seeking, vain, over-sensitive and fathomless. It has to be said that under most circumstances the first set of adjectives are the most appropriate, and that is because you keep control of the deeper side, refusing to allow it absolute control over your conscious life. You are able to get almost anything you want from life, but first you have to discover what that might be. The most important factor of all, however, is the way you can offer yourself, totally and without reservation to a needy world.

Self-sacrifice is a marvellous thing, but you can go too far on occasions. The furthest extreme for Scorpios here is a life that is totally dedicated to work and prayer. For the few this is admirable, for the still earth-based, less so. Finding a compromise is not easy as you are not always in touch with yourself. Feed the spiritual, curb the excesses, accept the need for luxury, and be happy.

Scorpio with Sagittarius Ascendant

There are many gains with this combination, and most of you reading this will already be familiar with the majority of them. Sagittarius offers a bright and hopeful approach to life, but may not always have the staying power and the patience to get what it really needs. Scorpio, on the other hand, can be too deep for its own good, is very self-seeking on occasions and extremely giving to others. Both the signs have problems when taken on their own, and, it has to be said, double the difficulties when they come together. But this is not usually the case. Invariably the presence of Scorpio slows down the over-quick responses of the Archer, whilst the inclusion of Sagittarius prevents Scorpio from taking itself too seriously.

Life is so often a game of extremes, when all the great spiritual masters of humanity have indicated that a 'middle way' is the path to choose. You have just the right combination of skills and mental faculties to find that elusive path, and can bring great joy to yourself and others as a result. Most of the time you are happy, optimistic, helpful and a joy to know. You have mental agility, backed up by a stunning intuition, which itself would rarely let you down. Keep a sense of proportion and understand that your depth of intellect is necessary to curb your flighty side.

Scorpio with Capricorn Ascendant

If patience, perseverance and a solid ability to get where you want to go are considered to be the chief components of a happy life, then you should be skipping about every day. Unfortunately this is not always the case and here we have two zodiac signs, both of which can be too deep for their own good. Both Scorpio and Capricorn are inclined to take themselves rather too seriously and your main lesson in life, and some would say the reason you have adopted this zodiac combination, is to 'lighten up'. If all that determination is pushed in the direction of your service to the world at large, you are seen as being one of the kindest people imaginable. This is really the only option for you, because if you turn this tremendous potential power inwards all the time you will become brooding, secretive and sometimes even selfish. Your eyes should be turned towards a needy humanity, which can be served with the dry but definite wit of Capricorn and the true compassion of Scorpio.

It is impossible with this combination to indicate what areas of life suit you the best. Certainly you adore luxury in all its forms, and yet you can get by with almost nothing. You desire travel, and at the same time love the comforts and stability of home. The people who know you best are aware that you are rather special. Listen to what they say.

Scorpio with Aquarius Ascendant

Here we have a combination that shows much promise and a flexibility that allows many changes in direction, allied to a power to succeed, sometimes very much against all the odds. Aquarius lightens the load of the Scorpio mind, turning the depths into potential and making intuitive foresight into a means for getting on in life. There are depths here, because even airy Aquarius isn't too easy to understand, and it is therefore a fact that some people with this combination will always be something of a mystery. However, even this fact can be turned to your advantage because it means that people will always be looking at you. Confidence is so often the key to success in life and the Scorpio–Aquarius mix offers this, or at least appears to do so. Even when this is not entirely the case, the fact that everyone around you believes it to be true is often enough.

You are usually good to know, and show a keen intellect and a deep intelligence, aided by a fascination for life that knows no bounds. When at your best you are giving, understanding, balanced and active. On those occasions when things are not going well for you, beware a stubborn streak and the need to be sensational. Keep it light and happy and you won't go far wrong. Most of you are very, very well loved.

Scorpio with Pisces Ascendant

You stand a chance of disappearing so deep into yourself that other people would need one of those long ladders that cave explorers use, just to find you. It isn't really your fault because both Scorpio and Pisces are Water signs, which are difficult to understand, and you have them both. But that doesn't mean that you should be content to remain in the dark, and the warmth of your nature is all you need to shine a light on the wonderful qualities you possess. But the primary word of warning is that you must put yourself on display and allow others to know what you are, before their appreciation of these facts becomes apparent.

As a server of the world you are second to none and it is hard to find a person with this combination who is not, in some way, looking out for the people around them. Immensely attractive to others, you are also one of the most sought-after lovers. Much of this has to do with your deep and abiding charm, but the air of mystery that surrounds you also helps. Some of you will marry too early, and end up regretting the fact, though the majority of people with Scorpio and Pisces will find the love they deserve in the end. You are able, just, firm but fair, though a sucker for a hard luck story and as kind as the day is long. It's hard to imagine how so many good points could be ignored by others.

Scorpio with Aries Ascendant

The two very different faces of Mars come together in this potent, magnetic and quite awe-inspiring combination. Your natural inclination is towards secrecy, and this fact, together with the natural attractions of the sensual Scorpio nature, makes you the object of great curiosity. This means that you will not go short of attention and should ensure that you are always being analysed by people who may never get to know you at all. At heart you prefer your own company, and yet life appears to find means to push you into the public gaze time and again. Most people with this combination ooze sex appeal and can use this fact as a stepping stone to personal success, yet without losing any integrity or loosening the cords of a deeply moralistic nature.

On those occasions when you do lose your temper, there isn't a character in the length and breadth of the zodiac who would have either the words or the courage to stand against the stream of invective that follows. On really rare occasions you might even scare yourself. A simple look is enough to show family members when you are not amused. Few people are left unmoved by your presence in their life.

Scorpio with Taurus Ascendant

The first, last and most important piece of advice for you is not to take yourself, or anyone else, too seriously. This might be rather a tall order because Scorpio intensifies the deeper qualities of Taurus and can make you rather lacking in the sense of humour that we all need to live our lives in this most imperfect of worlds. You are naturally sensual by nature. This shows itself in a host of ways. In all probability you can spend hours in the bath, love to treat yourself to good food and drink and take your greatest pleasure in neat and orderly surroundings. This can often alienate you from those who live in the same house because other people need to use the bathroom from time to time and they cannot remain tidy indefinitely.

You tend to worry a great deal about things which are really not too important, but don't take this statement too seriously or you will begin to worry about this fact too! You often need to lighten up and should always do your best to tell yourself that most things are not half so important as they seem to be. Be careful over the selection of a life partner and if possible choose someone who is naturally funny and who does not take life anywhere near as seriously as you are inclined to do. At work you are more than capable and in all probability everyone relies heavily on your wise judgements.

Scorpio with Gemini Ascendant

What you are and what you appear to be can be two entirely different things with this combination. Although you appear to be every bit as chatty and even as flighty as Gemini tends to be, nothing could be further from the truth. In reality you have many deep and penetrating insights, all of which are geared towards sorting out potential problems before they come along. Few people would have the ability to pull the wool over your eyes, and you show a much more astute face to the world than is often the case for Gemini taken on its own. The level of your confidence, although not earth-shattering, is much greater with this combination, and you would not be thwarted once you had made up your mind.

There is a slight danger here, however, because Gemini is always inclined to nerve problems of one sort or another. In the main these are slight and fleeting, though the presence of Scorpio can intensify reactions and heighten the possibility of depression, which would not be at all fortunate. The best way round this potential problem is to have a wealth of friends, plenty to do and the sort of variety in your life that suits your Mercury ruler. Financial success is not too difficult to achieve because you can easily earn money and then manage to hold on to it.

Scorpio with Cancer Ascendant

There are few more endearing zodiac combinations than this one. Both signs are Watery in nature and show a desire to work on behalf of humanity as a whole. The world sees you as being genuinely caring, full of sympathy for anyone in trouble and always ready to lend a hand when it is needed. You are a loyal friend, a great supporter of the oppressed and a lover of home and family. In a work sense you are capable, and command respect from your colleagues, even though this comes about courtesy of your quiet competence and not as a result of anything that you might happen to say.

But we should not get too carried away with external factors, or the way that others see you. Inside you are a boiling pool of emotion. You feel more strongly, love more deeply and hurt more fully than any other combination of the Water signs. Even those who think they know you really well would get a shock if they could take a stroll around the deeper recesses of your mind. Although these facts are true, they may be rather beside the point because it is a fact that the truth of your passion, commitment and deep convictions may only surface fully half a dozen times in your life. The fact is that you are a very private person at heart and you don't know how to be any other way.

Scorpio with Leo Ascendant

A Leo with intensity, that's what you are. You are mad about good causes and would argue the hind leg off a donkey in defence of your many ideals. If you are not out there saving the planet you could just be at home in the bath, thinking up the next way to save humanity from its own worst excesses. In your own life, although you love little luxuries, you are sparing and frugal, yet generous as can be to those you take to. It's a fact that you don't like everyone, and of course the same is true in reverse. It might be easier for you to understand why you can dislike than to appreciate the reverse side of the coin, for your pride can be badly dented on occasions. Scorpio brings a tendency to have down spells, though the fact that Leo is also strongly represented in your nature should prevent them from becoming a regular part of your life.

It is important for you to learn how to forgive and forget, and there isn't much point in bearing a grudge because you are basically too noble to do so. If something goes wrong, kiss the situation goodbye and get on with the next interesting adventure, of which there are many in your life. Stop–start situations sometimes get in the way, but there are plenty of people around who would be only too willing to lend a helping hand.

Scorpio with Virgo Ascendant

This is intensity carried through to the absolute. If you have a problem, it is that you fail to externalise all that is going on inside that deep, bubbling cauldron that is your inner self. Realising what you are capable of is not a problem; these only start when you have to make it plain to those around you what you want. Part of the reason for this is that you don't always understand yourself. You love intensely and would do absolutely anything for a person you are fond of, even though you might have to inconvenience yourself a great deal on the way. Relationships can cause you slight problems however, since you need to associate with people who at least come somewhere near to understanding what makes you tick. If you manage to bridge the gap between yourself and the world that constantly knocks on your door, you show yourself to be powerful, magnetic and compulsive.

There are times when you definitely prefer to stay quiet, though you do have a powerful ability to get your message across when you think it is necessary to do so. There are people around who might think that you are a push-over but they could easily get a shock when you sense that the time is right to answer back. You probably have a very orderly house and don't care for clutter of any sort.

Scorpio with Libra Ascendant

There is some tendency for you to be far more deep than the average Libran would appear to be and for this reason it is crucial that you lighten up from time to time. Every person with a Scorpio quality needs to remember that there is a happy and carefree side to all events and your Libran quality should allow you to bear this in mind. Sometimes you try to do too many things at the same time. This is fine if you take the casual overview of Libra, but less sensible when you insist on picking the last bone out of every potential, as is much more the case for Scorpio.

When worries come along, as they sometimes will, be able to listen to what your friends have to say and also realise that they are more than willing to work on your behalf, if only because you are so loyal to them. You do have a quality of self-deception, but this should not get in the way too much if you combine the instinctive actions of Libra with the deep intuition of your Scorpio component.

Probably the most important factor of this combination is your ability to succeed in a financial sense. You make a good manager, but not of the authoritarian sort. Jobs in the media or where you are expected to make up your mind quickly would suit you, because there is always an underpinning of practical sense that rarely lets you down.

THE MOON AND THE PART IT PLAYS IN YOUR LIFE

In astrology the Moon is probably the single most important heavenly body after the Sun. Its unique position, as partner to the Earth on its journey around the solar system, means that the Moon appears to pass through the signs of the zodiac extremely quickly. The zodiac position of the Moon at the time of your birth plays a great part in personal character and is especially significant in the build-up of your emotional nature.

Your Own Moon Sign

Discovering the position of the Moon at the time of your birth has always been notoriously difficult because tracking the complex zodiac positions of the Moon is not easy. This process has been reduced to three simple stages with our Lunar Tables. A breakdown of the Moon's zodiac positions can be found from page 35 onwards, so that once you know what your Moon Sign is, you can see what part this plays in the overall build-up of your personal character.

If you follow the instructions on the next page you will soon be able to work out exactly what zodiac sign the Moon occupied on the day that you were born and you can then go on to compare the reading for this position with those of your Sun sign and your Ascendant. It is partly the comparison between these three important positions that goes towards making you the unique individual you are.

HOW TO DISCOVER YOUR MOON SIGN

This is a three-stage process. You may need a pen and a piece of paper but if you follow the instructions below the process should only take a minute or so.

STAGE 1 First of all you need to know the Moon Age at the time of your birth. If you look at Moon Table 1, on page 33, you will find all the years between 1912 and 2010 down the left side. Find the year of your birth and then trace across to the right to the month of your birth. Where the two intersect you will find a number. This is the date of the New Moon in the month that you were born. You now need to count forward the number of days between the New Moon and your own birthday. For example, if the New Moon in the month of your birth was shown as being the 6th and you were born on the 20th, your Moon Age Day would be 14. If the New Moon in the month of your birth came after your birthday, you need to count forward from the New Moon in the previous month. Whatever the result, jot this number down so that you do not forget it.

STAGE 2 Take a look at Moon Table 2 on page 34. Down the left hand column look for the date of your birth. Now trace across to the month of your birth. Where the two meet you will find a letter. Copy this letter down alongside your Moon Age Day.

STAGE 3 Moon Table 3 on page 34 will supply you with the zodiac sign the Moon occupied on the day of your birth. Look for your Moon Age Day down the left hand column and then for the letter you found in Stage 2. Where the two converge you will find a zodiac sign and this is the sign occupied by the Moon on the day that you were born.

Your Zodiac Moon Sign Explained

You will find a profile of all zodiac Moon Signs on pages 35 to 38, showing in yet another way how astrology helps to make you into the individual that you are. In each daily entry of the Astral Diary you can find the zodiac position of the Moon for every day of the year. This also allows you to discover your lunar birthdays. Since the Moon passes through all the signs of the zodiac in about a month, you can expect something like twelve lunar birthdays each year. At these times you are likely to be emotionally steady and able to make the sort of decisions that have real, lasting value.

MOON TABLE 1

YEAR	SEP	OCT	NOV	YEAR	SEP	OCT	NOV	YEAR	SEP	OCT	NOV
1912	12	11	9	1945	6	6	4	1978	2	2/31	30
1913	30	29	28	1946	25	24	23	1979	21	20	19
1914	19	19	17	1947	14	14	12	1980	10	9	8
1915	9	8	7	1948	3	2	1	1981	28	27	26
1916	27	27	26	1949	23	21	20	1982	17	17	15
1917	15	15	14	1950	12	11	9	1983	7	6	4
1918	4	4	3	1951	1	1/30	29	1984	25	24	22
1919	23	23	22	1952	19	18	17	1985	14	14	12
1920	12	12	10	1953	8	8	6	1986	4	3	2
1921	2	1/30	29	1954	27	26	25	1987	23	22	21
1922	21	20	19	1955	16	15	14	1988	11	10	9
1923	10	10	8	1956	4	4	2	1989	29	29	28
1924	28	28	26	1957	23	23	21	1990	19	18	17
1925	18	17	16	1958	13	12	11	1991	8	8	6
1926	7	6	5	1959	3	2/31	30	1992	26	25	24
1927	25	25	24	1960	21	20	19	1993	16	15	14
1928	14	14	12	1961	10	9	8	1994	5	5	3
1929	3	2	1	1962	28	28	27	1995	24	24	22
1930	22	20	19	1963	17	17	15	1996	13	11	10
1931	12	11	9	1964	6	5	4	1997	2	2/31	30
1932	30	29	27	1965	25	24	22	1998	20	20	19
1933	19	19	17	1966	14	14	12	1999	9	9	8
1934	9	8	7	1967	4	3	2	2000	27	27	26
1935	27	27	26	1968	23	22	21	2001	17	17	16
1936	15	15	14	1969	11	10	9	2002	6	6	4
1937	4	4	3	1970	1	1/30	29	2003	26	25	24
1938	23	23	22	1971	19	19	18	2004	13	12	11
1939	13	12	11	1972	8	8	6	2005	3	2	1
1940	2	1/30	29	1973	27	26	25	2006	22	21	20
1941	21	20	19	1974	16	15	14	2007	12	11	9
1942	10	10	8	1975	5	5	3	2008	30	29	28
1943	29	29	27	1976	23	23	21	2009	19	18	17
1944	17	17	15	1977	13	12	11	2010	8	8	6

TABLE 2

DAY	OCT	NOV
1	a	e
2	a	e
3	a	e
4	b	f
5	b	f
6	b	f
7	b	f
8	b	f
9	b	f
10	b	f
11	b	f
12	b	f
13	b	g
14	d	g
15	d	g
16	d	g
17	d	g
18	d	g
19	d	g
20	d	g
21	d	g
22	d	g
23	d	i
24	e	i
25	e	i
26	e	i
27	e	i
28	e	i
29	e	i
30	e	i
31	e	–

MOON TABLE 3

M/D	a	b	d	e	f	g	i
0	LI	LI	LI	SC	SC	SC	SA
1	LI	LI	SC	SC	SC	SA	SA
2	LI	SC	SC	SC	SA	SA	CP
3	SC	SC	SC	SA	SA	CP	CP
4	SC	SA	SA	SA	CP	CP	CP
5	SA	SA	SA	CP	CP	AQ	AQ
6	SA	CP	CP	CP	AQ	AQ	AQ
7	SA	CP	CP	AQ	AQ	PI	PI
8	CP	CP	CP	AQ	PI	PI	PI
9	CP	AQ	AQ	AQ	PI	PI	AR
10	AQ	AQ	AQ	PI	AR	AR	AR
11	AQ	PI	PI	PI	AR	AR	TA
12	PI	PI	PI	AR	TA	TA	TA
13	PI	AR	PI	AR	TA	TA	GE
14	AR	AR	AR	TA	GE	GE	GE
15	AR	AR	AR	TA	TA	TA	GE
16	AR	AR	TA	TA	GE	GE	GE
17	AR	TA	TA	GE	GE	GE	CA
18	TA	TA	GE	GE	GE	CA	CA
19	TA	TA	GE	GE	CA	CA	CA
20	GE	GE	GE	CA	CA	CA	LE
21	GE	GE	CA	CA	CA	LE	LE
22	GE	CA	CA	CA	LE	LE	VI
23	CA	CA	CA	LE	LE	LE	VI
24	CA	CA	LE	LE	LE	VI	VI
25	CA	LE	LE	LE	VI	VI	LI
26	LE	LE	VI	VI	VI	LI	LI
27	LE	VI	VI	VI	LI	LI	SC
28	VI	VI	VI	LI	LI	LI	SC
29	VI	VI	LI	LI	LI	SC	SC

AR = Aries, TA = Taurus, GE = Gemini, CA = Cancer, LE = Leo, VI = Virgo, LI = Libra, SC = Scorpio, SA = Sagittarius, CP = Capricorn, AQ = Aquarius, PI = Pisces

MOON SIGNS

Moon in Aries

You have a strong imagination, courage, determination and a desire to do things in your own way and forge your own path through life.

Originality is a key attribute; you are seldom stuck for ideas although your mind is changeable and you could take the time to focus on individual tasks. Often quick-tempered, you take orders from few people and live life at a fast pace. Avoid health problems by taking regular time out for rest and relaxation.

Emotionally, it is important that you talk to those you are closest to and work out your true feelings. Once you discover that people are there to help, there is less necessity for you to do everything yourself.

Moon in Taurus

The Moon in Taurus gives you a courteous and friendly manner, which means you are likely to have many friends.

The good things in life mean a lot to you, as Taurus is an Earth sign that delights in experiences which please the senses. Hence you are probably a lover of good food and drink, which may in turn mean you need to keep an eye on the bathroom scales, especially as looking good is also important to you.

Emotionally you are fairly stable and you stick by your own standards. Taureans do not respond well to change. Intuition also plays an important part in your life.

Moon in Gemini

You have a warm-hearted character, sympathetic and eager to help others. At times reserved, you can also be articulate and chatty: this is part of the paradox of Gemini, which always brings duplicity to the nature. You are interested in current affairs, have a good intellect, and are good company and likely to have many friends. Most of your friends have a high opinion of you and would be ready to defend you should the need arise. However, this is usually unnecessary, as you are quite capable of defending yourself in any verbal confrontation.

Travel is important to your inquisitive mind and you find intellectual stimulus in mixing with people from different cultures. You also gain much from reading, writing and the arts but you do need plenty of rest and relaxation in order to avoid fatigue.

Moon in Cancer

The Moon in Cancer at the time of birth is a fortunate position as Cancer is the Moon's natural home. This means that the qualities of compassion and understanding given by the Moon are especially enhanced in your nature, and you are friendly and sociable and cope well with emotional pressures. You cherish home and family life, and happily do the domestic tasks. Your surroundings are important to you and you hate squalor and filth. You are likely to have a love of music and poetry.

Your basic character, although at times changeable like the Moon itself, depends on symmetry. You aim to make your surroundings comfortable and harmonious, for yourself and those close to you.

Moon in Leo

The best qualities of the Moon and Leo come together to make you warm-hearted, fair, ambitious and self-confident. With good organisational abilities, you invariably rise to a position of responsibility in your chosen career. This is fortunate as you don't enjoy being an 'also-ran' and would rather be an important part of a small organisation than a menial in a large one.

You should be lucky in love, and happy, provided you put in the effort to make a comfortable home for yourself and those close to you. It is likely that you will have a love of pleasure, sport, music and literature. Life brings you many rewards, most of them as a direct result of your own efforts, although you may be luckier than average and ready to make the best of any situation.

Moon in Virgo

You are endowed with good mental abilities and a keen receptive memory, but you are never ostentatious or pretentious. Naturally quite reserved, you still have many friends, especially of the opposite sex. Marital relationships must be discussed carefully and worked at so that they remain harmonious, as personal attachments can be a problem if you do not give them your full attention.

Talented and persevering, you possess artistic qualities and are a good homemaker. Earning your honours through genuine merit, you work long and hard towards your objectives but show little pride in your achievements. Many short journeys will be undertaken in your life.

Moon in Libra

With the Moon in Libra you are naturally popular and make friends easily. People like you, probably more than you realise, you bring fun to a party and are a natural diplomat. For all its good points, Libra is not the most stable of astrological signs and, as a result, your emotions can be a little unstable too. Therefore, although the Moon in Libra is said to be good for love and marriage, your Sun sign and Rising sign will have an important effect on your emotional and loving qualities.

You must remember to relate to others in your decision-making. Co-operation is crucial because Libra represents the 'balance' of life that can only be achieved through harmonious relationships. Conformity is not easy for you because Libra, an Air sign, likes its independence.

Moon in Scorpio

Some people might call you pushy. In fact, all you really want to do is to live life to the full and protect yourself and your family from the pressures of life. Take care to avoid giving the impression of being sarcastic or impulsive and use your energies wisely and constructively.

You have great courage and you invariably achieve your goals by force of personality and sheer effort. You are fond of mystery and are good at predicting the outcome of situations and events. Travel experiences can be beneficial to you.

You may experience problems if you do not take time to examine your motives in a relationship, and also if you allow jealousy, always a feature of Scorpio, to cloud your judgement.

Moon in Sagittarius

The Moon in Sagittarius helps to make you a generous individual with humanitarian qualities and a kind heart. Restlessness may be intrinsic as your mind is seldom still. Perhaps because of this, you have a need for change that could lead you to several major moves during your adult life. You are not afraid to stand your ground when you know your judgement is right, you speak directly and have good intuition.

At work you are quick, efficient and versatile and so you make an ideal employee. You need work to be intellectually demanding and do not enjoy tedious routines.

In relationships, you anger quickly if faced with stupidity or deception, though you are just as quick to forgive and forget. Emotionally, there are times when your heart rules your head.

Moon in Capricorn

The Moon in Capricorn makes you popular and likely to come into the public eye in some way. The watery Moon is not entirely comfortable in the Earth sign of Capricorn and this may lead to some difficulties in the early years of life. An initial lack of creative ability and indecision must be overcome before the true qualities of patience and perseverance inherent in Capricorn can show through.

You have good administrative ability and are a capable worker, and if you are careful you can accumulate wealth. But you must be cautious and take professional advice in partnerships, as you are open to deception. You may be interested in social or welfare work, which suit your organisational skills and sympathy for others.

Moon in Aquarius

The Moon in Aquarius makes you an active and agreeable person with a friendly, easy-going nature. Sympathetic to the needs of others, you flourish in a laid-back atmosphere. You are broad-minded, fair and open to suggestion, although sometimes you have an unconventional quality which others can find hard to understand.

You are interested in the strange and curious, and in old articles and places. You enjoy trips to these places and gain much from them. Political, scientific and educational work interests you and you might choose a career in science or technology.

Money-wise, you make gains through innovation and concentration and Lunar Aquarians often tackle more than one job at a time. In love you are kind and honest.

Moon in Pisces

You have a kind, sympathetic nature, somewhat retiring at times, but you always take account of others' feelings and help when you can.

Personal relationships may be problematic, but as life goes on you can learn from your experiences and develop a better understanding of yourself and the world around you.

You have a fondness for travel, appreciate beauty and harmony and hate disorder and strife. You may be fond of literature and would make a good writer or speaker yourself. You have a creative imagination and may come across as an incurable romantic. You have strong intuition, maybe bordering on a mediumistic quality, which sets you apart from the mass. You may not be rich in cash terms, but your personal gifts are worth more than gold.

SCORPIO IN LOVE

Discover how compatible you are with people from the same and other parts of the zodiac. Five stars equals a match made in heaven!

Scorpio meets Scorpio

Scorpio is deep, complex and enigmatic, traits which often lead to misunderstanding with other zodiac signs, so a double Scorpio match can work well because both parties understand one another. They will allow each other periods of silence and reflection but still be willing to help, advise and support when necessary. Their relationship may seem odd to others but that doesn't matter if those involved are happy. All in all, an unusual but contented combination. Star rating: *****

Scorpio meets Sagittarius

Sagittarius needs constant stimulation and loves to be busy from dawn till dusk which may mean that it feels rather frustrated by Scorpio. Scorpions are hard workers, too, but they are also contemplative and need periods of quiet which may mean that they appear dull to Sagittarius. This could lead to a gulf between the two which must be overcome. With time and patience on both sides, this can be a lucrative encounter and good in terms of home and family. A variable alliance. Star rating: ***

Scorpio meets Capricorn

Lack of communication is the governing factor here. Neither of this pair are renowned communicators and both need a partner to draw out their full verbal potential. Consequently, Scorpio may find Capricorn cold and unapproachable while Capricorn could find Scorpio dark and brooding. Both are naturally tidy and would keep a pristine house but great effort and a mutual goal is needed on both sides to overcome the missing spark. A good match on the financial side, but probably not an earthshattering personal encounter. Star rating: **

Scorpio meets Aquarius

This is a promising and practical combination. Scorpio responds well to Aquarius' exploration of its deep nature and so this shy sign becomes lighter, brighter and more inspirational. Meanwhile, Aquarians are rarely as sure of themselves as they like to appear and are reassured by Scorpio's steady and determined support. Both signs want to be kind to the other which is a basis for a relationship that should be warm most of the time and extremely hot occasionally. Star rating: ****

Scorpio meets Pisces

If ever there were two zodiac signs that have a total rapport, it has to be Scorpio and Pisces. They share very similar needs: they are not gregarious and are happy with a little silence, good music and time to contemplate the finer things in life, and both are attracted to family life. Apart, they can have a tendency to wander in a romantic sense, but this is reduced when they come together. They are deep, firm friends who enjoy each other's company and this must lead to an excellent chance of success. These people are surely made for each other! Star rating: *****

Scorpio meets Aries

There can be great affection here, even if the two signs are so very different. The common link is the planet Mars, which plays a part in both these natures. Although Aries is, outwardly, the most dominant, Scorpio people are among the most powerful to be found anywhere. This quiet determination is respected by Aries. Aries will satisfy the passionate side of Scorpio, particularly with instruction from Scorpio. There are mysteries here which will add spice to life. The few arguments that do occur are likely to be awe-inspiring. Star rating: ****

Scorpio meets Taurus

Scorpio is deep – very deep – which may be a problem, because Taurus doesn't wear its heart on its sleeve either. It might be difficult for this pair to get together, because neither is naturally inclined to make the first move. Taurus stands in awe of the power and intensity of the Scorpio mind, while the Scorpion is interested in the Bull's affable and friendly qualities, so an enduring relationship could be forged if the couple ever get round to talking. Both are lovers of home and family, which will help to cement a relationship. Star rating: **

Scorpio meets Gemini

There could be problems here. Scorpio is one of the deepest and least understood of all the zodiac signs, which at first seems like a challenge to intellectual Gemini, who thinks it can solve anything. But the deeper the Gemini digs, the further down Scorpio goes. Meanwhile, Scorpio may be finding Gemini thoughtless, shallow and even downright annoying. Gemini is often afraid of Scorpio's perception and strength, together with the sting in the Scorpion's tail. Anything is possible, but the outlook for this match is less than promising. Star rating: **

Scorpio meets Cancer

This match is potentially a great success, a fact which is often a mystery to astrologers. Some feel it is due to the compatibility of the Water element, but it could also come from a mixture of similarity and difference in the personalities. Scorpio is partly ruled by Mars, which gives it a deep, passionate, dominant and powerful side. Cancerians generally like and respect this amalgam, and recognise something there that they would like to adopt themselves. On the other side of the coin, Scorpio needs love and emotional security which Cancer offers generously. Star rating: *****

Scorpio meets Leo

Stand back and watch the sparks fly! Scorpio has the deep sensitivity of a Water sign but it is also partially ruled by Fire planet Mars, from which it draws great power, and Leo will find that difficult. Leo loves to take charge and really hates to feel psychologically undermined, which is Scorpio's stock-in-trade. Scorpio may find Leo's ideals a little shallow, which will be upsetting to the Lion. Anything is possible, but this possibility is rather slimmer than most. Star rating: **

Scorpio meets Virgo

There are one or two potential difficulties here, but there is also a meeting point from which to overcome them. Virgo is very caring and protective, a trait which Scorpio understands and even emulates. Scorpio will impress Virgo with its serious side. Both signs are consistent, although also sarcastic. Scorpio may uncover a hidden passion in Virgo which all too often lies deep within its Earth-sign nature. Material success is very likely, with Virgo taking the lion's share of the domestic chores and family responsibilities. Star rating: ***

Scorpio meets Libra

Many astrologers have reservations about this match because, on the surface, the signs are so different. However, this couple may find fulfilment because these differences mean that their respective needs are met. Scorpio needs a partner to lighten the load, which won't daunt Libra, while Libra looks for a steadfast quality which it doesn't possess, but which Scorpio can supply naturally. Financial success is possible because they both have good ideas and back them up with hard work and determination. All in all, a promising outlook. Star rating: ****

VENUS: THE PLANET OF LOVE

If you look up at the sky around sunset or sunrise you will often see Venus in close attendance to the Sun. It is arguably one of the most beautiful sights of all and there is little wonder that historically it became associated with the goddess of love. But although Venus does play an important part in the way you view love and in the way others see you romantically, this is only one of the spheres of influence that it enjoys in your overall character.

Venus has a part to play in the more cultured side of your life and has much to do with your appreciation of art, literature, music and general creativity. Even the way you look is responsive to the part of the zodiac that Venus occupied at the start of your life, though this fact is also down to your Sun sign and Ascending sign. If, at the time you were born, Venus occupied one of the more gregarious zodiac signs, you will be more likely to wear your heart on your sleeve, as well as to be more attracted to entertainment, social gatherings and good company. If on the other hand Venus occupied a quiet zodiac sign at the time of your birth, you would tend to be more retiring and less willing to shine in public situations.

It's good to know what part the planet Venus plays in your life for it can have a great bearing on the way you appear to the rest of the world and since we all have to mix with others, you can learn to make the very best of what Venus has to offer you.

One of the great complications in the past has always been trying to establish exactly what zodiac position Venus enjoyed when you were born because the planet is notoriously difficult to track. However, we have solved that problem by creating a table that is exclusive to your Sun sign, which you will find on the following page.

Establishing your Venus sign could not be easier. Just look up the year of your birth on the next page and you will see a sign of the zodiac. This was the sign that Venus occupied in the period covered by your sign in that year. If Venus occupied more than one sign during the period, this is indicated by the date on which the sign changed, and the name of the new sign. For instance, if you were born in 1950, Venus was in Libra until the 28th October, after which time it was in Scorpio. If you were born before 28th October your Venus sign is Libra, if you were born on or after 28th October, your Venus sign is Scorpio. Once you have established the position of Venus at the time of your birth, you can then look in the pages which follow to see how this has a bearing on your life as a whole.

1912 SCORPIO / 24.10 SAGITTARIUS / 18.11 CAPRICORN
1913 LIBRA / 14.11 SCORPIO
1914 SAGITTARIUS / 16.11 SCORPIO
1915 SCORPIO / 9.11 SAGITTARIUS
1916 VIRGO / 3.11 LIBRA
1917 SAGITTARIUS / 7.11 CAPRICORN
1918 LIBRA / 30.10 SCORPIO
1919 VIRGO / 9.11 LIBRA
1920 SCORPIO / 24.10 SAGITTARIUS / 17.11 CAPRICORN
1921 LIBRA / 14.11 SCORPIO
1922 SAGITTARIUS / 16.11 SCORPIO
1923 SCORPIO / 9.11 SAGITTARIUS
1924 VIRGO / 3.11 LIBRA
1925 SAGITTARIUS / 7.11 CAPRICORN
1926 LIBRA / 29.10 SCORPIO
1927 VIRGO / 10.11 LIBRA
1928 SAGITTARIUS / 17.11 CAPRICORN
1929 LIBRA / 13.11 SCORPIO
1930 SAGITTARIUS / 16.11 SCORPIO
1931 SCORPIO / 8.11 SAGITTARIUS
1932 VIRGO / 2.11 LIBRA
1933 SAGITTARIUS / 7.11 CAPRICORN
1934 LIBRA / 29.10 SCORPIO
1935 VIRGO / 10.11 LIBRA
1936 SAGITTARIUS / 16.11 CAPRICORN
1937 LIBRA / 13.11 SCORPIO
1938 SAGITTARIUS / 16.11 SCORPIO
1939 SCORPIO / 7.11 SAGITTARIUS
1940 VIRGO / 2.11 LIBRA
1941 SAGITTARIUS / 7.11 CAPRICORN
1942 LIBRA / 28.10 SCORPIO
1943 VIRGO / 10.11 LIBRA
1944 SAGITTARIUS / 16.11 CAPRICORN
1945 LIBRA / 13.11 SCORPIO
1946 SAGITTARIUS / 16.11 SCORPIO
1947 SCORPIO / 6.11 SAGITTARIUS
1948 VIRGO / 1.11 LIBRA
1949 SAGITTARIUS / 6.11 CAPRICORN
1950 LIBRA / 28.10 SCORPIO
1951 VIRGO / 10.11 LIBRA
1952 SAGITTARIUS / 16.11 CAPRICORN
1953 LIBRA / 12.11 SCORPIO
1954 SAGITTARIUS / 28.10 SCORPIO
1955 SCORPIO / 6.11 SAGITTARIUS
1956 VIRGO / 1.11 LIBRA
1957 SAGITTARIUS / 6.11 CAPRICORN
1958 LIBRA / 27.10 SCORPIO
1959 VIRGO / 10.11 LIBRA
1960 SAGITTARIUS / 15.11 CAPRICORN
1961 LIBRA / 12.11 SCORPIO
1962 SAGITTARIUS / 28.10 SCORPIO
1963 SCORPIO / 5.11 SAGITTARIUS
1964 VIRGO / 31.10 LIBRA
1965 SAGITTARIUS / 6.11 CAPRICORN
1966 LIBRA / 27.10 SCORPIO
1967 VIRGO / 10.11 LIBRA
1968 SAGITTARIUS / 15.11 CAPRICORN
1969 LIBRA / 11.11 SCORPIO
1970 SAGITTARIUS / 28.10 SCORPIO
1971 SCORPIO / 4.11 SAGITTARIUS
1972 VIRGO / 31.10 LIBRA
1973 SAGITTARIUS / 6.11 CAPRICORN
1974 LIBRA / 26.10 SCORPIO
1975 VIRGO / 9.11 LIBRA
1976 SAGITTARIUS / 15.11 CAPRICORN
1977 LIBRA / 11.11 SCORPIO
1978 SAGITTARIUS / 28.10 SCORPIO
1979 SCORPIO / 4.11 SAGITTARIUS
1980 VIRGO / 30.10 LIBRA
1981 SAGITTARIUS / 5.11 CAPRICORN
1982 LIBRA / 26.10 SCORPIO
1983 VIRGO / 9.11 LIBRA
1984 SAGITTARIUS / 14.11 CAPRICORN
1985 LIBRA / 10.11 SCORPIO
1986 SAGITTARIUS / 28.10 SCORPIO
1987 SCORPIO / 3.11 SAGITTARIUS
1988 VIRGO / 30.10 LIBRA
1989 SAGITTARIUS / 5.11 CAPRICORN
1990 LIBRA / 25.10 SCORPIO
1991 VIRGO / 9.11 LIBRA
1992 SAGITTARIUS / 14.11 CAPRICORN
1993 LIBRA / 10.11 SCORPIO
1994 SAGITTARIUS / 28.10 SCORPIO
1995 SCORPIO / 3.11 SAGITTARIUS
1996 VIRGO / 29.10 LIBRA
1997 SAGITTARIUS / 5.11 CAPRICORN
1998 LIBRA / 25.10 SCORPIO
1999 VIRGO / 9.11 LIBRA
2000 SAGITTARIUS / 14.11 CAPRICORN
2001 LIBRA / 10.11 SCORPIO
2002 SAGITTARIUS / 28.10 SCORPIO
2003 SCORPIO / 3.11 SAGITTARIUS
2004 VIRGO / 29.10 LIBRA
2005 SAGITTARIUS / 5.11 CAPRICORN
2006 LIBRA / 25.10 SCORPIO
2007 VIRGO / 9.11 LIBRA
2008 SAGITTARIUS / 14.11 CAPRICORN
2009 LIBRA / 10.11 SCORPIO
2010 SAGITTARIUS / 28.10 SCORPIO

VENUS THROUGH THE ZODIAC SIGNS

Venus in Aries

Amongst other things, the position of Venus in Aries indicates a fondness for travel, music and all creative pursuits. Your nature tends to be affectionate and you would try not to create confusion or difficulty for others if it could be avoided. Many people with this planetary position have a great love of the theatre, and mental stimulation is of the greatest importance. Early romantic attachments are common with Venus in Aries, so it is very important to establish a genuine sense of romantic continuity. Early marriage is not recommended, especially if it is based on sympathy. You may give your heart a little too readily on occasions.

Venus in Taurus

You are capable of very deep feelings and your emotions tend to last for a very long time. This makes you a trusting partner and lover, whose constancy is second to none. In life you are precise and careful and always try to do things the right way. Although this means an ordered life, which you are comfortable with, it can also lead you to be rather too fussy for your own good. Despite your pleasant nature, you are very fixed in your opinions and quite able to speak your mind. Others are attracted to you and historical astrologers always quoted this position of Venus as being very fortunate in terms of marriage. However, if you find yourself involved in a failed relationship, it could take you a long time to trust again.

Venus in Gemini

As with all associations related to Gemini, you tend to be quite versatile, anxious for change and intelligent in your dealings with the world at large. You may gain money from more than one source but you are equally good at spending it. There is an inference here that you are a good communicator, via either the written or the spoken word, and you love to be in the company of interesting people. Always on the look-out for culture, you may also be very fond of music, and love to indulge the curious and cultured side of your nature. In romance you tend to have more than one relationship and could find yourself associated with someone who has previously been a friend or even a distant relative.

Venus in Cancer

You often stay close to home because you are very fond of family and enjoy many of your most treasured moments when you are with those you love. Being naturally sympathetic, you will always do anything you can to support those around you, even people you hardly know at all. This charitable side of your nature is your most noticeable trait and is one of the reasons why others are naturally so fond of you. Being receptive and in some cases even psychic, you can see through to the soul of most of those with whom you come into contact. You may not commence too many romantic attachments but when you do give your heart, it tends to be unconditionally.

Venus in Leo

It must become quickly obvious to almost anyone you meet that you are kind, sympathetic and yet determined enough to stand up for anyone or anything that is truly important to you. Bright and sunny, you warm the world with your natural enthusiasm and would rarely do anything to hurt those around you, or at least not intentionally. In romance you are ardent and sincere, though some may find your style just a little overpowering. Gains come through your contacts with other people and this could be especially true with regard to romance, for love and money often come hand in hand for those who were born with Venus in Leo. People claim to understand you, though you are more complex than you seem.

Venus in Virgo

Your nature could well be fairly quiet no matter what your Sun sign might be, though this fact often manifests itself as an inner peace and would not prevent you from being basically sociable. Some delays and even the odd disappointment in love cannot be ruled out with this planetary position, though it's a fact that you will usually find the happiness you look for in the end. Catapulting yourself into romantic entanglements that you know to be rather ill-advised is not sensible, and it would be better to wait before you committed yourself exclusively to any one person. It is the essence of your nature to serve the world at large and through doing so it is possible that you will attract money at some stage in your life.

Venus in Libra

Venus is very comfortable in Libra and bestows upon those people who have this planetary position a particular sort of kindness that is easy to recognise. This is a very good position for all sorts of friendships and also for romantic attachments that usually bring much joy into your life. Few individuals with Venus in Libra would avoid marriage and since you are capable of great depths of love, it is likely that you will find a contented personal life. You like to mix with people of integrity and intelligence but don't take kindly to scruffy surroundings or work that means getting your hands too dirty. Careful speculation, good business dealings and money through marriage all seem fairly likely.

Venus in Scorpio

You are quite open and tend to spend money quite freely, even on those occasions when you don't have very much. Although your intentions are always good, there are times when you get yourself in to the odd scrape and this can be particularly true when it comes to romance, which you may come to late or from a rather unexpected direction. Certainly you have the power to be happy and to make others contented on the way, but you find the odd stumbling block on your journey through life and it could seem that you have to work harder than those around you. As a result of this, you gain a much deeper understanding of the true value of personal happiness than many people ever do, and are likely to achieve true contentment in the end.

Venus in Sagittarius

You are lighthearted, cheerful and always able to see the funny side of any situation. These facts enhance your popularity, which is especially high with members of the opposite sex. You should never have to look too far to find romantic interest in your life, though it is just possible that you might be too willing to commit yourself before you are certain that the person in question is right for you. Part of the problem here extends to other areas of life too. The fact is that you like variety in everything and so can tire of situations that fail to offer it. All the same, if you choose wisely and learn to understand your restless side, then great happiness can be yours.

Venus in Capricorn

The most notable trait that comes from Venus in this position is that it makes you trustworthy and able to take on all sorts of responsibilities in life. People are instinctively fond of you and love you all the more because you are always ready to help those who are in any form of need. Social and business popularity can be yours and there is a magnetic quality to your nature that is particularly attractive in a romantic sense. Anyone who wants a partner for a lover, a spouse and a good friend too would almost certainly look in your direction. Constancy is the hallmark of your nature and unfaithfulness would go right against the grain. You might sometimes be a little too trusting.

Venus in Aquarius

This location of Venus offers a fondness for travel and a desire to try out something new at every possible opportunity. You are extremely easy to get along with and tend to have many friends from varied backgrounds, classes and inclinations. You like to live a distinct sort of life and gain a great deal from moving about, both in a career sense and with regard to your home. It is not out of the question that you could form a romantic attachment to someone who comes from far away or be attracted to a person of a distinctly artistic and original nature. What you cannot stand is jealousy, for you have friends of both sexes and would want to keep things that way.

Venus in Pisces

The first thing people tend to notice about you is your wonderful, warm smile. Being very charitable by nature you will do anything to help others, even if you don't know them well. Much of your life may be spent sorting out situations for other people, but it is very important to feel that you are living for yourself too. In the main, you remain cheerful, and tend to be quite attractive to members of the opposite sex. Where romantic attachments are concerned, you could be drawn to people who are significantly older or younger than yourself or to someone with a unique career or point of view. It might be best for you to avoid marrying whilst you are still very young.

SCORPIO: 2009 DIARY PAGES

October
2009

1 THURSDAY *Moon Age Day 12 Moon Sign Pisces*

Even if your daily life is somewhat less orderly than you would wish, you needn't let this be too much of a problem, particularly if you make use of the humour you have available. The first day of October has potential to be a somewhat mixed bag, but there should be enough going on to keep you happy, as well as the chance to attract plenty of compliments!

2 FRIDAY *Moon Age Day 13 Moon Sign Pisces*

Social matters should now be a breeze, and you have what it takes to bring out the best in others. As the weekend approaches you may decide to throw in your lot with people who want to have a good time, and this could involve you stretching your own personality to accommodate theirs. Romance should be high on your Friday agenda.

3 SATURDAY *Moon Age Day 14 Moon Sign Pisces*

There are signs that you may become easily distracted, and that concentration might be difficult. There are probably things occupying your mind that really have no business to be there, but it could be difficult to dump them in the delete bin. Maybe you are trying too hard? Why not just enjoy what the day has to offer in a social sense?

4 SUNDAY *Moon Age Day 15 Moon Sign Aries*

You now have the ability to make a warm and enriching connection to others, and you will rarely have been more loved than could turn out to be the case today. If people care for you just the way you are, ask yourself whether there is any point in trying to alter yourself in any way. The spotlight is on movement and activity later in the day.

5 MONDAY *Moon Age Day 16 Moon Sign Aries*

Today has potential to be a slightly negative interlude, partly because of the approaching lunar low. With the Sun now in your solar twelfth house it is also possible you could be led up the garden path regarding some issue you thought you understood perfectly. This is not a bad day, but extra care will probably be necessary.

6 TUESDAY *Moon Age Day 17 Moon Sign Taurus*

The lunar low supports a tendency for you to over-stress your importance in specific issues, and as a result you might come unstuck. It would be better today to listen to what others are saying and to learn from past mistakes. Even if you are not pushing your life forward in any specific way right now, you can still be very circumspect and quite shrewd.

7 WEDNESDAY *Moon Age Day 18 Moon Sign Taurus*

Trends do nothing to increase your general level of self-confidence, though at the back of your mind you should still be sure of yourself and may be anxious to prove your instincts out there in the wide world. If this isn't possible for the moment, it's worth keeping your powder dry and laying down a few ground rules for later on.

8 THURSDAY *Moon Age Day 19 Moon Sign Gemini*

An ideal day for facing potential challenges, and you have what it takes to deal with them head-on. You can make sure today is better in a number of ways, not least by being more communicative and willing to step out of the shadows. Knowing that you are important to family and friends can bring you great joy, so why not find out how they really see you?

9 FRIDAY *Moon Age Day 20 Moon Sign Gemini*

Although you have scope to move forward move progressively in certain areas of your life, there may still be a slight reticence when it comes to proving yourself in a work setting. Perhaps you believe that others are more capable than you are. Putting in some extra effort is just one of the ways that you can prove this isn't the case.

10 SATURDAY *Moon Age Day 21 Moon Sign Gemini*

A strong sense of personal freedom is now starting to prevail, though your present twelfth-house Sun might discourage you from throwing caution to the wind in the way you would wish. Maybe this isn't a bad thing because there are occasions when Scorpio becomes too radical and too determined for its own eventual good.

11 SUNDAY *Moon Age Day 22 Moon Sign Cancer*

The position of Mercury offers the chance to use a greater level of intuition and to recognise how others are likely to react under almost any given circumstance. Don't knock this ability, because it will not let you down. In affairs of the heart it's time to show just how sincere you can be, and you might even decide to really floor someone with affection!

12 MONDAY *Moon Age Day 23 Moon Sign Cancer*

You can now take advantage of one of the best days of the month with regard to financial issues. It is clearly time to put certain matters into a better working order and to forge ahead. When the practicalities of the day are out of the way, there is much to be said for choosing to spend as much time as possible with people you care for deeply.

13 TUESDAY *Moon Age Day 24 Moon Sign Leo*

A certain deep-seated sense of isolation could well keep coming and going for a while yet, and this is because of the Sun, out there in your solar twelfth house. It does little to assist your efforts to get onside with specific people, and can even make personal attachments slightly more remote than you would wish. Patience is the key.

14 WEDNESDAY *Moon Age Day 25 Moon Sign Leo*

Be prepared to make contact with any new people who emerge onto the social scene, some of whom could be right up your street. You don't make personal friends easily, but when you do you can ensure that they stick around for a long time. Such is likely to be the case around now, so why not cast your line and reel in a couple of new buddies?

15 THURSDAY *Moon Age Day 26 Moon Sign Virgo*

Trends highlight problems regarding information you have been awaiting for quite some time. Rather than panicking about this situation, your best response would simply be to demonstrate some Scorpio patience. In affairs of the heart you can afford to show your true colours, though you shouldn't pretend you are in love if this isn't the case.

16 FRIDAY *Moon Age Day 27 Moon Sign Virgo*

This is a good time to do some deep thinking with regard to your life in an overall sense – which is one of the blessings of a twelfth-house Sun. At the same time a sense of isolation is possible, though you need to consider whether it is you who is building the walls yourself. In three or four days a new phase is on offer, so struggle on if that's what it takes.

17 SATURDAY *Moon Age Day 28 Moon Sign Libra*

Some personal matters could seem like genuinely hard work, particularly if the people you are dealing with don't seem to be doing a great deal to help themselves. Routine chores could well seem tedious, and there is nothing wrong with deciding to ring the changes and do something absolutely different if you can today.

18 SUNDAY *Moon Age Day 0 Moon Sign Libra*

Scorpio thrives on competition and never turns away from a good fight. That's fine, but you could be up against a genuine adversary at the moment and it isn't going to help your self-confidence if you fail to come up to scratch. A little persuasion is worth any amount of argument today, and you should still manage to prove your point.

19 MONDAY *Moon Age Day 1 Moon Sign Scorpio*

With the Sun moving towards your solar first house and with the Moon in your zodiac sign, your sights should be set on a more progressive future. Today the lunar high offers you greater incentives, better communication skills and positive contacts with the world at large. The world is your oyster, and you can certainly gain support for your wildest plans.

20 TUESDAY *Moon Age Day 2 Moon Sign Scorpio*

You can now press forward with significant confidence towards any goals and objectives that have been shelved for some time. This has potential to be the most confident part of the year, and it begins with the opportunity to attract greater support, even from those people you thought for sure could be against your hopes, wishes and desires.

21 WEDNESDAY *Moon Age Day 3 Moon Sign Sagittarius*

Improving the emotional quality of your life is what seems important today. The Sun has not quite reached your first house yet, and so for today at least you have a chance to look deep inside yourself. That's fine for now, but at any moment the world could explode with new changes, and there probably won't be too much time for contemplation.

22 THURSDAY *Moon Age Day 4 Moon Sign Sagittarius*

You can take advantage of some important financial news at any time now. For this reason it is vitally important that you pay attention, especially at work. You can capitalise on information that you discover, and could make yourself better off as a result. A day to get friends to lend their support to your plans and follow your lead.

23 FRIDAY *Moon Age Day 5 Moon Sign Sagittarius*

The swift influence of the Moon in your solar third house can assist you to be much better at expressing yourself in an emotional sense. If there are things that have needed to be said for a while, now is the time to get them out in the open. It's worth getting to grips with anything you have been putting off, and making the most of praise from colleagues.

24 SATURDAY *Moon Age Day 6 Moon Sign Capricorn*

The Sun is now firmly placed in your solar first house, offering a month-long period during which you can make all the incentives your own. You have what it takes to make the world a better place, particularly if you allow your natural Scorpio foreboding to take a holiday. The days are drawing in, but the call of the great outdoors is still there.

25 SUNDAY *Moon Age Day 7 Moon Sign Capricorn*

Trends assist you to be at your most imaginative, at least when it comes to ambitious ideas. Another factor to bear in mind at the moment is that your creative traits are emphasised. You can develop a picture of anything in your mind and then play it out in the real world. Nothing is more effective than the true Scorpio imagination.

26 MONDAY *Moon Age Day 8 Moon Sign Aquarius*

If you have been put under pressure regarding a domestic issue, now is the time for a good heart-to-heart talk in order to sort things out once and for all. You should find it easier than ever to come to terms with the ideas and opinions of your partner, and have a chance to show yourself to be a loyal and supportive lover. Just wait for the results.

27 TUESDAY *Moon Age Day 9 Moon Sign Aquarius*

Self-motivation is the key at the moment, and you have the ability to show great strength of character. This is nothing new for Scorpio, but you can now demonstrate your skills in a friendlier and more social way. As a result you can enhance your popularity, and can gain the support of others as you move towards your cherished objectives.

28 WEDNESDAY *Moon Age Day 10 Moon Sign Aquarius*

When it comes to career aims you now have the warrior spirit about you. Trends encourage you to pursue your goals with all available energy and in such a way that nobody should stand in your way. You can show even your superiors how positive you are, and elicit their support on the way. After all, your success will reflect favourably on them too.

29 THURSDAY *Moon Age Day 11 Moon Sign Pisces*

You have scope to display a more dynamic personality all the time, and the Moon, presently in your solar fifth house, offers even greater incentives and new opportunities. Taken together these positive planetary trends introduce you to one of the most dynamic phases you will encounter this year. Now is the time to shine!

30 FRIDAY *Moon Age Day 12 Moon Sign Pisces*

Make good use of your radiant personality, and in particular your very broad smile. If you are funny, others will want to be your friend, and this might even include those who haven't always supported or liked you in the past. Letting bygones be bygones, although never easy for Scorpio, turns out to be the best course of action.

31 SATURDAY *Moon Age Day 13 Moon Sign Aries*

Be prepared to capitalise on opportunities linked to people from the past who turn up again now, especially those who have been living at a great distance from you for quite a while. If you have kept in touch with such an individual, don't be surprised if they arrive at your home or contact you soon. This is not a day for routines, so alter everything you can.

November
2009

1 SUNDAY *Moon Age Day 14 Moon Sign Aries*

The first day of November supports a very positive frame of mind and a strong desire to succeed at every level of life that proves to be possible. Even if it takes you slightly longer to do certain things today, in the main you can demonstrate the capable and very creative side of your nature. A short quiet interlude is at hand, but for today you need to shine.

2 MONDAY *Moon Age Day 15 Moon Sign Aries*

If things you have been working very hard to achieve now become stuck fast, your best response is simply to watch and wait. The approaching lunar low supports this far more circumspect approach, but it does at least offer you the chance to take stock, which in the middle of such a hectic period probably turns out to be a good thing.

3 TUESDAY *Moon Age Day 16 Moon Sign Taurus*

This may not be the best of days, particularly if you decide to blame absolutely everyone when things go wrong – except yourself. Nevertheless, the positive planets are so strong that you should be able to keep a smile on your face, and that proves to be all-important. If you can laugh at your blunders you can persuade the world to smile with you.

4 WEDNESDAY *Moon Age Day 17 Moon Sign Taurus*

Mercury is now close to the Sun in your solar first house, and as the lunar low fades, the positives influences get better and better. What this means is that your communications skills are emphasised, assisting your efforts to get important people to take your side in an issue or dispute. You also have scope to solve a problem from long ago.

5 THURSDAY *Moon Age Day 18 Moon Sign Gemini*

At work you will be suited to anything that offers you a significant challenge. If you aren't happy with a routine sort of day, you might even decide to deliberately upset the applecart in order to sort out the ensuing chaos. Most important of all is the way you use your natural cheerfulness to inspire everyone and maintain your popularity.

6 FRIDAY *Moon Age Day 19 Moon Sign Gemini*

Today the focus is on your great ability to express yourself and your superb command of the language. These could come in useful if anyone crosses you deliberately, and in most situations you can get your point of view accepted. You have scope to improve family relationships and to offer sound advice to younger people if they need it.

7 SATURDAY *Moon Age Day 20 Moon Sign Cancer*

Now you can afford to be a freedom-loving type who is active and enterprising in every phase of life. If you are not a weekend worker, there is much to be said for putting on your hiking boots, enlisting your partner or a friend, and walking to the top of a large hill. Fresh air and open spaces are the key to fulfilment today.

8 SUNDAY *Moon Age Day 21 Moon Sign Cancer*

Business and financial matters offer opportunities for success, though of course these may not apply on a Sunday. Whatever you decide to take on can be undertaken in a flash, and with great good humour. Bear in mind that the greater the level of popularity you achieve, the more thinly you may have to spread yourself today.

9 MONDAY *Moon Age Day 22 Moon Sign Leo*

You should feel quite optimistic about life at the moment and ought to be doing all you can at the start of this week to improve your lot in a practical and a financial sense. Now is an ideal time to clear up any misunderstandings, and to pursue efforts to get on better with anyone who has really annoyed you in the past.

10 TUESDAY *Moon Age Day 23 Moon Sign Leo*

Your communicative abilities are still stimulated by the position of Mercury in your solar chart, encouraging you to talk to just about anyone who is willing to listen. This isn't entirely typical of Scorpio, so in some ways you are on unknown ground, but there won't be much doubt about the way you can persuade people generally to listen to you.

11 WEDNESDAY *Moon Age Day 24 Moon Sign Virgo*

In career matters especially you have a great deal of energy at your disposal, and in a general sense you can now project the sort of courage that is typical of Scorpio. Your strength lies in your willingness to stand up for the underdog, and your determination to do what is necessary to show those around you how much concern you have for their welfare.

12 THURSDAY *Moon Age Day 25 Moon Sign Virgo*

Your diplomatic style can help you to win friends and influence people – which again is a slight departure from the way Scorpio sometimes behaves. With your intuition turned up high you can assess the way people are likely to react to you before you fire off, and this can be a great help in the longer term. Romance is in the air for some Scorpios.

13 FRIDAY *Moon Age Day 26 Moon Sign Libra*

With swift Mercury now in your own zodiac sign you have what it takes to be spontaneous in your thinking and your actions. Today is about responding quickly to all situations, and not waiting around to be asked when there are possible gains to be made. This is an excellent time for picking up new information and for using it to your advantage.

14 SATURDAY *Moon Age Day 27 Moon Sign Libra*

You can demonstrate an enthusiastic and even lordly approach to life whilst the Sun predominates so much in your chart. Ambitious schemes are right up your street at the moment, and it's worth spending at least part of this weekend putting some of them into action. Be prepared to listen to grouses from family members, and to try to sort things out.

15 SUNDAY *Moon Age Day 28 Moon Sign Scorpio*

The first day of the lunar low has potential to be one of the best days of the month, because just about everything is working to your advantage from an astrological point of view. Your level of available good luck should be much higher than usual, allowing you to approach situations with a great deal of confidence and a determination to win.

16 MONDAY *Moon Age Day 29 Moon Sign Scorpio*

Your spirit of independence remains highlighted, as does your great determination to tackle any issues that have dogged you in the past. Today offers you scope to improve your circumstances and also the lives of people who rely heavily upon you. Standing up for your rights should be no problem, particularly if you show both courage and patience.

17 TUESDAY *Moon Age Day 0 Moon Sign Scorpio*

The Moon is still in your zodiac sign, as is the Sun. On the day of the New Moon you might find that some of the benefits come along despite you. There could be just a slight feeling that someone else is running the show, and even if this makes you feel somewhat uncomfortable, the results should be the same – a happy and fulfilling day.

18 WEDNESDAY *Moon Age Day 1 Moon Sign Sagittarius*

You can quite clearly make the most of your engaging approach to life by spreading an atmosphere of harmony and understanding wherever you go. This is not universally the case for Scorpio, which can be quite disruptive sometimes. As a result, you can increase your level of popularity, particularly if you can get friends to pay you some attention.

19 THURSDAY *Moon Age Day 2 Moon Sign Sagittarius*

The emphasis is on taking life more seriously for the next few days, and on considering the sort of impression you want to make on the world at large. This is something you needn't worrying too much about right now, because things are so good astrologically. Keep abreast of local news and current affairs in order to make gains.

20 FRIDAY *Moon Age Day 3 Moon Sign Capricorn*

Short journeys should suit you down to the ground, and you will probably not take kindly to being constrained in any way. Now is the time to show the world the most versatile side of your nature and to make the best of impressions when you are at work. Don't be afraid to lay on the compliments with a trowel for colleagues and bosses.

21 SATURDAY *Moon Age Day 4 Moon Sign Capricorn*

Romance and social engagements can offer you the chance to keep smiling this weekend, and you may also be anxious to get out of the house and into situations you find stimulating and exciting. If you are generally some sort of Cinderella, it's time to get out that pumpkin and phone your Fairy Godmother. What the heck – go to the ball!

22 SUNDAY *Moon Age Day 5 Moon Sign Capricorn*

A day to slow life down just a little and think about spending more time in the company of your nearest and dearest. Of course this doesn't mean you have to sit around knitting. You could find something exciting to do that includes family members. Anyone who doesn't want to be involved can please themselves!

23 MONDAY *Moon Age Day 6 Moon Sign Aquarius*

It would be more than worthwhile today to put in an extra bit of effort in order to secure your financial future. Before taking any decisions, you would be wise to make sure that all the preparations have been done. It's time to get your thinking cap on, because this would be an ideal opportunity to sort such things out.

24 TUESDAY *Moon Age Day 7 Moon Sign Aquarius*

When it comes to your finances today could be a good time to experiment, even if you only do so in a theoretical sense. Even if you are not generally given to wild schemes or madcap enterprises, there might be something on offer now that appeals to you in a certain way. Caution is fine, but you also need to back your hunches now and again.

25 WEDNESDAY *Moon Age Day 8 Moon Sign Pisces*

While the emphasis is on fun and leisure, why not take a day's holiday from work and get together with a friend? You can afford to do what you fancy, whether that's a shopping trip or a good old chat. Failing this you can make a good impression on colleagues right now, though not by talking about the same old things. Sort out your correspondence.

26 THURSDAY *Moon Age Day 9 Moon Sign Pisces*

You are now in a position to spend a great deal of time and effort improving your finances. Your ability to make monetary gains is well starred, though it may be a fact of life that for every amount coming in, there is a bill to be paid. This needn't bother you too much if you are determined to make full use of present planetary trends.

27 FRIDAY *Moon Age Day 10 Moon Sign Pisces*

Newer and better developments are on offer for most Scorpios, though seeing the way ahead may not always be that easy. There are chances to make positive gains in friendships, and romance is also favoured at the moment. Why not get in touch with someone you haven't seen for a while and swap a few tales? It is important to be sociable now.

28 SATURDAY *Moon Age Day 11 Moon Sign Aries*

In terms of work you now have a good sense of contingencies, and can use your organisational skills to the full across the weekend. Making minor adjustments is essential, though tampering with things that are going well enough on their own is certainly not. Creature comforts could take on a greater importance as the winter advances.

29 SUNDAY *Moon Age Day 12 Moon Sign Aries*

You might decide to rest today because before the day is out the lunar low will be upon you. Beware of taking on matters that are going to take a great deal of effort to sort out, and be willing to leave specific tasks to family members and friends. You are best off now in an organisational role – telling everyone else what they should be doing!

30 MONDAY *Moon Age Day 13 Moon Sign Taurus*

The lunar low may slow down the start of the week, but you needn't let it get in your way to any great extent. It is possible that you could feel just slightly under the weather, though this really depends on how much you are willing to take a back seat and meditate more. What really matters is that you avoid pushing yourself too hard.

December
2009

1 TUESDAY *Moon Age Day 14 Moon Sign Taurus*

The first day of December brings a time of fluctuating moods. As a result there may be a little restlessness to cope with, not to mention a tendency to retreat from issues you don't like the look of. Hard-and-fast decisions regarding the future are best left until tomorrow, and for now there's nothing wrong with simply treading water for a while.

2 WEDNESDAY *Moon Age Day 15 Moon Sign Gemini*

You have sufficient enthusiasm at your disposal to encourage a more positive attitude within your own mind today. The lunar low is out of the way and some fairly positive influences will be taking its place. Even if you don't have everything in position for making that essential leap forward, much of what you need is to hand. You simply have to look.

3 THURSDAY *Moon Age Day 16 Moon Sign Gemini*

When it comes to sorting out your finances, you can't really expect a better set of planetary positions than the ones that surround you at the moment. Be prepared to get others to take on a more responsible attitude, which will in turn allow you to inculcate them into your own plans. Friends especially might be finding new ways to please you.

4 FRIDAY *Moon Age Day 17 Moon Sign Cancer*

Freedom is the best key to happiness today, which is why you will probably hate being fettered in any way. Scorpio has an opportunity to break out, and some of the people you deal with in a daily sense may find your present attitude difficult to assess or to deal with. Don't be afraid to show the world how wonderfully silly you can be now!

5 SATURDAY *Moon Age Day 18 Moon Sign Cancer*

A fairly challenging period is on the way with regard to your career, though for many Scorpio subjects thoughts on such matters can wait for a couple of days. The weekend offers you scope to do something really off the wall and amuse everyone by playing the fool. It's not a common feature in the lives of many Scorpios, but it can be refreshing.

6 SUNDAY *Moon Age Day 19 Moon Sign Leo*

On the one hand you may feel instinctively that this is a good period to buckle down and do some work, but on the other hand you probably don't want to be practical. If there is a compromise, it could be hard to find. Bear in mind that the atypical approach that is supported by current trends could be difficult for others to understand and deal with.

7 MONDAY *Moon Age Day 20 Moon Sign Leo*

So much more can be done now by following your intuition and by making sure you are well aware of everything that is going on around you. If you make the most of today, under most circumstances you are unlikely to miss a trick, and you can also secure a good deal of support from the sort of people who are always true to their word.

8 TUESDAY *Moon Age Day 21 Moon Sign Virgo*

When it comes to professional developments you would be wise not to over-estimate yourself and your capacities today. The support of others can still be important, and if you go it alone too much at the moment you could find yourself facing problems. From a romantic point of view this is an ideal time to address the needs of your partner.

9 WEDNESDAY *Moon Age Day 22 Moon Sign Virgo*

You now have the potential to gain through co-operative ventures with a business partner or a really good friend. Shared ideas hold the best potential, and there should be little to hold you back except perhaps your own lack of confidence. You can only do really well if you are sure of what you are doing and why you are undertaking it.

10 THURSDAY *Moon Age Day 23 Moon Sign Libra*

Your ability to communicate remains highlighted. Now that Mercury is in your solar third house it is the things you say to others that can make all the difference. If you still don't want to go it alone as much as Scorpio sometimes does, there is much to be said for relying on friends and colleagues. This won't always be a comfortable position.

11 FRIDAY *Moon Age Day 24 Moon Sign Libra*

Quiet solitude and contemplation could work well for you and this is because the Moon is in your solar twelfth house ahead of the lunar high. Rewards are available if you succeed in getting really close to loved ones now, and you have what it takes to make the best of impressions when you are dealing with family members.

12 SATURDAY *Moon Age Day 25 Moon Sign Libra*

Things could still be fairly quiet, which might make this an ideal time to get out a pen and paper and jot down all those last-minute details for Christmas. After today trends indicate a busier interlude, and you may not have as much time to think as you do right now. Your creative potential is extremely well marked for the next few days.

13 SUNDAY *Moon Age Day 26 Moon Sign Scorpio*

During this phase of rising self-confidence you have the opportunity to get most plans and schemes to take off more or less the way you had hoped. Outside of work a socially minded approach works best, and for some Scorpio individuals the festive season is already underway. Today would be excellent for taking almost any sort of journey.

14 MONDAY *Moon Age Day 27 Moon Sign Scorpio*

When it comes to general good luck and being in the right place at the best time it appears that nobody can touch you today. All you need is self-belief and the opportunity to show what you are capable of achieving. This is a time when you can influence the ideas and opinions of others, to your mutual benefit.

15 TUESDAY *Moon Age Day 28 Moon Sign Sagittarius*

You can now afford to be more individualistic and to show your competitive side. Moreover, trends encourage you to take on very ambitious projects in your drive to succeed, and the thought of the responsibility involved shouldn't bother you one bit. The only thing you need that might not be present in great measure is patience.

16 WEDNESDAY *Moon Age Day 0 Moon Sign Sagittarius*

Even if you manage to attract the money you need today, holding onto cash may be more difficult – which let's face it isn't so surprising anyway at this time of year. A more circumspect approach when buying gifts would be no bad thing. Instead of opting for what you see first, it's worth doing a little searching to make sure you get good value.

17 THURSDAY *Moon Age Day 1 Moon Sign Capricorn*

This is a time to capitalise on those clever, sharp insights of the type that Scorpio often has. You have scope to achieve a genuine breakthrough with regard to a plan that has been on hold, and to ensure that other people are now more willing to back you. In particular, there are gains to be made if you manage to get superiors on your side.

18 FRIDAY *Moon Age Day 2 Moon Sign Capricorn*

Now is an ideal time for professional wheeling and dealing. You can afford to give yourself credit for your solid intuition and to back your hunches in projects that you want to get finished before Christmas. Speaking of the festivities, you might well be dragged into social events you hadn't planned for. Simply smile and get involved.

19 SATURDAY *Moon Age Day 3 Moon Sign Capricorn*

You can benefit from moneymaking schemes, just as long as you know that you are not about to be duped. Things work out best when the ideas are yours and when it is you who lays down the ground rules. This is just as true in a social sense, particularly if you aren't too impressed with the way other people are planning their social gatherings.

20 SUNDAY *Moon Age Day 4 Moon Sign Aquarius*

The present position of the Moon offers you an opportunity to look again at the past, so you might decide to get out all those old decorations or those cards from people who don't figure in your life any more. In a general sense the focus is on remaining active, though you may decide to retreat from time to time if you feel your position to be threatened.

21 MONDAY *Moon Age Day 5 Moon Sign Aquarius*

In a financial sense getting your own way could be slightly easier today, and you have what it takes to bring other people round to your specific point of view. There is much to be said for a slightly more frugal approach, particularly if you are spending far more than is good for you. There are ways and means round everything, as you will discover.

22 TUESDAY *Moon Age Day 6 Moon Sign Pisces*

It is safe to say today works best if you get yourself in the driving seat where practical or professional matters are concerned, and you can steal a march on others, especially if everyone else has already stopped work ahead of Christmas. The key is to remain committed to the task at hand, and that is what enables you to get ahead.

23 WEDNESDAY *Moon Age Day 7 Moon Sign Pisces*

Today is ideal for organising social outings or accepting an invitation to some sort of pre-Christmas gathering. At the same time you need to be sure that all details are sorted out before you drop the reins of responsibility yourself. Getting other people to fulfil their obligations may not be easy – especially where family matters are concerned.

24 THURSDAY *Moon Age Day 8 Moon Sign Pisces*

A phase of increased curiosity is on offer, urging you to look under every stone you come across today. This is no bad thing, because you could discover something that is to your distinct advantage. You can tap into slightly more luck than usual today, especially if you have bought raffle tickets or made a minor speculation.

25 FRIDAY *Moon Age Day 9 Moon Sign Aries*

You should enjoy being on the go for Christmas Day. In fact, you may well be here, there and everywhere. The position of Mercury makes this an ideal time for being amongst family and friends, and you have scope to be the life and soul of the party. Be prepared to put any tendency towards nostalgia on the back burner and enjoy the moment.

26 SATURDAY *Moon Age Day 10 Moon Sign Aries*

Boxing Day should represent another good time to show everyone just how joyful and sharing you can be. Venus highlights the sweeter side of your nature and assists you to offer those timely compliments that others want to hear so much. This has potential to be the most romantic day you will encounter during the length of the holidays.

27 SUNDAY *Moon Age Day 11 Moon Sign Taurus*

Your level of energy in a general sense may not be at its best as the lunar low sets in. For today and tomorrow you might be happier to relax and to spend most of your time with those you feel closest to in an emotional sense. However, your ingenuity is still good, and you can use it to find the solution to any sort of puzzle or problem.

28 MONDAY *Moon Age Day 12 Moon Sign Taurus*

You may find it wisest to allow your partner or other family members to make most of the decisions today, whilst you enjoy a well-earned rest. Today responds best if you attend to minor jobs and deal with short-term considerations. Looking too far ahead could give you a headache. It's not worth getting depressed over issues that haven't happened yet.

29 TUESDAY *Moon Age Day 13 Moon Sign Taurus*

As today wears on you can demonstrate your sharp mind and the fact that you excel at problem solving of just about any sort. If you have a very big task in front of you, your best approach is to break it down into smaller components. Progress is possible if you remain optimistic and more than certain regarding your own abilities.

30 WEDNESDAY *Moon Age Day 14 Moon Sign Gemini*

There is extra happiness and confidence available as far as your social life is concerned. Even casual conversations can help you to reach major conclusions, and you should be happiest when you know you are making a good impression. Short journeys could be important today because they offer new incentives on which you can capitalise.

31 THURSDAY *Moon Age Day 15 Moon Sign Gemini*

The spotlight today is on your sense of personal freedom. If you decide to make any resolutions, don't be afraid to make them with your personal choices in mind. What may not work out well today are those situations in which others think they know you better than they really do. Try to curb impatience and to enjoy the day.

SCORPIO:
2010 DIARY PAGES

SCORPIO: 2010 IN BRIEF

You need to be quite positive in your approach at the very start of the year and should not allow yourself to be diverted from your path during January and February. There are complications to deal with, but in the main you will be able to get on well, especially in practical matters. Personal attachments can throw up slight complications from time to time.

March and April should find you in a more positive frame of mind and better able to forge new paths for yourself, especially in a professional sense. You will also be very sociable and less inclined to stick with your own company than might sometimes be the case. In terms of romance you should be really on form, and your love life is likely to be much warmer than the weather. You could be choosing this time to make a break with convention.

As the summer arrives you will be getting itchy feet and will need to get out and about more than has been the case earlier. Any sort of journey is likely to suit you fine, whether it is for business or pleasure. Intuition plays a big part in your life during May and June, so much so that you probably won't make any major decisions without it. Friends may be fickle, but can also be funny and extremely helpful as far as you are concerned.

July and August are months of change and diversity for you. Almost anything can be turned on its head, though always in a positive way. In a professional sense you could be thinking about changing your job and you will also be keen to seek out fresh fields and pastures new as much as proves to be possible. In fact very little is impossible for you at this time and you show how positive you can be.

As the year moves on, September and October bring you closer to your astrological home and offer a greater sense of security. You may not be moving about quite as much, but then most of your really good times will be at home or with close friends. You can increase your income at this time and should be on fine form socially and romantically. A new and important friendship is likely to start during this period.

November and December should prove to be inspiring, warm and generally happy. Contentment is something you always crave but sometimes it is better if life shakes you up a little because then you try harder. November is the best month for money, which you will quite happily spend in December. You have scope to make this a very family-motivated Christmas and New Year.

January 2010

1 FRIDAY ☿ *Moon Age Day 16 Moon Sign Cancer*

You can afford to start the year with fairly strident opinions, supported by the Moon in your solar ninth house. Although most of what you are thinking and saying makes great sense, bear in mind the possibility that you might cause unintended offence. It's worth toning your opinions down somewhat if you want to avoid problems.

2 SATURDAY ☿ *Moon Age Day 17 Moon Sign Cancer*

There are now definite gains to be made in communication matters as new contacts and meetings with old friends allow you to widen your scope for the future. It's time to find all sorts of different people who can contribute to your life's rich variety, possibly even some individuals you haven't exactly seen eye-to-eye with in the past.

3 SUNDAY ☿ *Moon Age Day 18 Moon Sign Leo*

Trends suggest that everyday mundane matters may not be of interest to you at present, mainly because of the position of little Mercury in your solar chart. Anything that makes life more interesting should be considered, and today in particular may be a chance for you to come face to face with a situation that holds great promise for the longer-term future.

4 MONDAY ☿ *Moon Age Day 19 Moon Sign Leo*

Most social developments should be going rather well, though there may be some slight complications as far as your personal life is concerned. By all means seek out new incentives that could revolutionise your life in the weeks or months to come, but for the moment as far as work is concerned there's nothing wrong with more of the same.

5 TUESDAY ☿ *Moon Age Day 20 Moon Sign Virgo*

Look out for important signposts to success. Being a Scorpio you can draw on great patience when necessary, and should be quite happy to watch and wait, planning carefully and getting things sorted out as required. In conversation a sensitive approach works best, and you can afford to put yourself out to help your friends.

6 WEDNESDAY ☿ *Moon Age Day 21 Moon Sign Virgo*

With the Moon now moving into your solar twelfth house you need to be ready to respond to a more inward-looking phase. Your power and influence over others may be less well accented, and you might have to make do with second-best in some situations. Scorpio could also become more of a home bird during the next couple of days.

7 THURSDAY ☿ *Moon Age Day 22 Moon Sign Libra*

Despite any tendency to withdraw, you can still keep your mind looking outward. This is a legacy of a third-house Sun and it could prove to be your best saving grace at the moment. Even if you aren't in the market for strenuous activity, your mind has potential to be working ten to the dozen and to come up with some amazing ideas.

8 FRIDAY ☿ *Moon Age Day 23 Moon Sign Libra*

As today progresses you have scope to make life busier and busier. A little reluctance to be drawn forth from your own little cocoon is only natural, but by the afternoon you should be able to get fully back in gear and ready to take part. Things that friends have to say could enable you to throw new light on a specific issue.

9 SATURDAY ☿ *Moon Age Day 24 Moon Sign Scorpio*

The Moon has now moved into your own sign of Scorpio and this brings you to the part of the month known as the lunar high. During the next couple of days you should be on fine form and you will have what it takes to turn heads wherever you go. Motivation is strong, and you should also be able to make use of all your energy at this time.

10 SUNDAY ☿ *Moon Age Day 25 Moon Sign Scorpio*

Today is about how willing you are to take big chances and to be more assertive when you are dealing with issues you see as being important for the future. It's time to get Lady Luck on your side and to identify what you need to do in order to get what you want from life. Be prepared to seek some timely assistance from friends.

11 MONDAY ☿ *Moon Age Day 26 Moon Sign Sagittarius*

The need for caution at work looms large. Being in a big hurry and wanting to get on with specific jobs is fine, though it's worth remembering that those around you may disagree, or may not be ready. A degree of patience is called for, though that might not be easy to muster under present trends. Compromise is the key at the moment.

12 TUESDAY ☿ *Moon Age Day 27 Moon Sign Sagittarius*

The spotlight is now on higher learning and the pursuit of culture. The idealistic side of your nature is enhanced, and you won't be inclined to accept anything shabby or suspect. It's possible that not everyone can live up to your expectations of them, though you can also be quite funny at the moment, and can use this trait to defuse any awkward situations.

13 WEDNESDAY ☿ *Moon Age Day 28 Moon Sign Sagittarius*

Once again intellectual interests will help you to get the most from life and you have everything you need to solve puzzles and mysteries that have been around for quite some time. The answers you seek now stand out in stark relief from the background of life, and you can certainly impress others with your ability to sort things out.

14 THURSDAY ☿ *Moon Age Day 29 Moon Sign Capricorn*

Venus is now in your solar third house, assisting you to clear up problems from the past and to use your charm to defuse potential difficulties. News that you can discover today should be quite inspiring, and even if there are interruptions to be dealt with, this is one day during which you have a real opportunity to move forward.

15 FRIDAY ☿ *Moon Age Day 0 Moon Sign Capricorn*

It might be slightly more difficult today to focus on issues that you know to be of the greatest importance. If situations look fuzzy round the edges and if you can see no clear answers, you need to be prepared to be quite original in your thinking. You don't necessarily have to work everything out for yourself if you can seek help from a good friend.

16 SATURDAY ☿ *Moon Age Day 1 Moon Sign Aquarius*

Some of your duties to the outside world could now be less evident, particularly if you don't allow yourself to get quite as involved as would normally be the case. It's time to relax, and to make domestic issues more significant than your efforts out there in the wider world. Why not put your feet up and enjoy the warmth of your own hearth?

17 SUNDAY *Moon Age Day 2 Moon Sign Aquarius*

There ought to be plenty to keep you interested today, though that doesn't mean you have to make waves. On the contrary, a better option would be to adopt an attitude that says 'anything for a peaceful life'. Rather than this making you a more boring person, you can ensure that the reverse is true. It's all about increasing your popularity.

18 MONDAY *Moon Age Day 3 Moon Sign Aquarius*

Professional challenges are par for the course, but you have what it takes to take these in your stride. Today works best if you manage to be neither too pushy nor too quiet, and you can use this interlude to seek opportunities to make new friends. This might not be an outstanding day, but you can make it comfortable, especially if you keep your nature well balanced.

19 TUESDAY *Moon Age Day 4 Moon Sign Pisces*

Love and romantic attachments generally can become an obsession unless you exercise a degree of care. Beware of allowing any form of envy or jealousy to cloud your judgement, and do what you can to show how forgiving you can be. This should be a good time to bury the hatchet and to reach new understandings with others.

20 WEDNESDAY *Moon Age Day 5 Moon Sign Pisces*

Your home environment, together with your friends, should be enough for you at this time. There is little reason at present to try to break down barriers or prove how dynamic you are capable of being. This has potential to be another of those quiet days that epitomise this period and which offer you the chance to do yourself a lot of good in the longer term.

21 THURSDAY *Moon Age Day 6 Moon Sign Aries*

Trends assist you to function independently today, and you shouldn't require too much in the way of reassurance on a moment-by-moment basis. Once you have made up your mind to a particular course of action, why change it? Bear in mind that this might make you seem slightly intransigent when seen through the eyes of colleagues.

22 FRIDAY *Moon Age Day 7 Moon Sign Aries*

The Sun is now in your solar fourth house, encouraging you to make your home your main focus. Scorpio cares a great deal for the domestic side of life in any case, though you can now afford to allow your nearest and dearest to do things in their own way to a greater extent than usual. A day to avoid arguments like the plague!

23 SATURDAY *Moon Age Day 8 Moon Sign Aries*

You have a chance to slow things down somewhat as the day advances, and you may well remain quite immune to the sort of issues that normally get you motivated. There are planetary reasons why this is the case, though these probably won't become fully obvious until tomorrow. For the moment you need to be circumspect but always optimistic.

24 SUNDAY *Moon Age Day 9 Moon Sign Taurus*

Now the Moon has moved into your opposite zodiac sign of Taurus, and this heralds the two- or three-day period known as the lunar low. This is not a time for dynamic actions but rather a period during which you have an opportunity to rest and reflect. Any form of gambling is best avoided, and this is not a good time for commitments of any kind.

25 MONDAY *Moon Age Day 10 Moon Sign Taurus*

If you find yourself running out of steam at any stage today, your best response might be to allow others to take the strain whilst you rest and reflect on issues that could demand your attention later. It would be very easy to argue for your limitations at the moment, though it isn't really necessary to do so. Be prepared to wait and see.

26 TUESDAY *Moon Age Day 11 Moon Sign Gemini*

Domestic and family ties now fall under the spotlight and you may be pleased to know that the Moon has moved on and away from Taurus. This allows a more optimistic outlook and an interlude when you should be less inclined to see potential pitfalls and happy to create some fun around you. Steady actions are the order of the day.

27 WEDNESDAY *Moon Age Day 12 Moon Sign Gemini*

You can now gain from looking carefully at potential problems, rather than by wading in and taking actions that are not advisable. The adage 'fools rush in where angels fear to tread' is quite relevant to Scorpio on occasions, but you needn't let this be the case under present trends. Romance is well starred, and it's all about finding exactly the right amorous words.

28 THURSDAY *Moon Age Day 13 Moon Sign Cancer*

There are signs that your career life is epitomised at the moment by a desire to be out there at the front. That's fine, just as long as you can back up your hunches with concrete action. If you know you cannot, it would be better to wait and see. You can afford to be defensive of anyone you think is getting a raw deal, even if this means putting yourself out.

29 FRIDAY *Moon Age Day 14 Moon Sign Cancer*

This is an ideal time for remaining on the move and for making the very best of any travel opportunities that come your way. It's time to broaden your horizons as much as possible, since you could soon become bored if you decided to stay in the same place all the time. You have scope to bring new friends into your life at this stage.

30 SATURDAY *Moon Age Day 15 Moon Sign Leo*

You have what it takes to increase your profile in a number of different ways, and needn't allow endless chores to prevent you from doing what seems most appealing. The weekend offers a chance to get out and about and mix with as many different sorts of people as you can. Group activities are favoured, particularly if you can be in charge.

31 SUNDAY *Moon Age Day 16 Moon Sign Leo*

A marvellous time is on offer as far as your home life is concerned, but that needn't restrict you to staying around at home. This is an ideal time for trips, especially those you make in the company of your partner or family members. Having fun should be a big part of this particular Sunday, so get wrapped up against the cold and get out into the world.

February
2010

1 MONDAY *Moon Age Day 17 Moon Sign Virgo*

A change for the better is now within your grasp, and this could be easier to achieve if you make full use of teamwork and general co-operation with those around you. The weather outside might not be very good, but that shouldn't stop you being sunny and cheerful. With plenty to do and a smile on your face you can begin February on a positive note.

2 TUESDAY *Moon Age Day 18 Moon Sign Virgo*

The present position of Mercury enhances your curiosity and encourages you to look under every stone on your journey through life. For some Scorpios there may even be a few mysteries to solve, and it's worth keeping your detective hat on throughout most of today. All matters concerning communication are well accented now.

3 WEDNESDAY *Moon Age Day 19 Moon Sign Libra*

It is important for you to remain connected to the past as well as the present because Scorpio dwells in both. This tendency is much enhanced at this time, and you need to avoid losing contact with people or situations that were formerly very important to you. All the same, you need to remember that you can't bring back what has gone and it's pointless to try.

4 THURSDAY *Moon Age Day 20 Moon Sign Libra*

Some of the concrete achievements you are seeking may be difficult for you to attain under present trends. You might even manage to get ninety-nine percent of what you are chasing, but the elusive one percent remains theoretical. Don't worry about this, because nothing is lost, you can simply postpone it until another day.

5 FRIDAY *Moon Age Day 21 Moon Sign Scorpio*

The Moon is back in your zodiac sign and now you can really achieve favoured objectives. You have what it takes to get things done in a percentage of the time they would usually take, and you can make full use of your golden touch when you are dealing with those around you. Part of the result should be increased popularity, even with people you barely know.

6 SATURDAY *Moon Age Day 22 Moon Sign Scorpio*

New ideas can be given the go ahead, and you might even have energy to spare, no matter how busy you decide to be. If you are willing to be the one who makes the running, you can also make the rules, and for a Scorpio that is vitally important. Although you are usually careful not to speculate too much you may be inclined to do so today.

7 SUNDAY *Moon Age Day 23 Moon Sign Scorpio*

For the third day running the Moon shines down favourably upon you. There is much to be said for focusing on family members today and for choosing to have a good time in the company of people you love. Your general good luck continues, perhaps persuading you to take the sort of chances you would normally avoid.

8 MONDAY *Moon Age Day 24 Moon Sign Sagittarius*

Ideas and information become central to your strategy and you can forge ahead as a result of your own efforts, whilst at the same time co-operating fully with people who think along the same lines as you do. In almost every way you now have what it takes to make significant progress, but beware of being overcautious in matters of the heart.

9 TUESDAY *Moon Age Day 25 Moon Sign Sagittarius*

With Venus in your solar fourth house this is a favourable time for all home-based matters and family relationships. This assists you to reach new understandings with anyone you haven't seen eye to eye with recently, and to leave old issues firmly behind you. A forward-looking approach works best and helps your popularity in a social sense.

10 WEDNESDAY *Moon Age Day 26 Moon Sign Capricorn*

It is now more important than ever to recognise your roots and to connect fully with aspects of your past. At the same time you should be constantly looking forward, because there is just a slight tendency for you to get stuck with issues that do need to be changed. Getting onside with colleagues could also prove to be important today.

11 THURSDAY *Moon Age Day 27 Moon Sign Capricorn*

A more exciting social life becomes possible as Venus moves into your solar fifth house around now. Your strength lies in your ability to turn on the charm and to get people to notice you much more than they might usually be inclined to do. By all means remain generally active, and even sporting, though a cautious attitude works well in business.

12 FRIDAY *Moon Age Day 28 Moon Sign Aquarius*

Trends offer you a surplus of energy for business matters, though you might be slightly less inclined to socialise today and across the weekend. It isn't about being any less friendly, rather that you may have personal issues to address. This is also an ideal interlude to commit yourself to aspects of your home life and to any changes you want to make.

13 SATURDAY *Moon Age Day 29 Moon Sign Aquarius*

'Never a dull moment' should be the motto for today, and never more so than at home. You have scope to make this an enjoyable phase as far as your personal life is concerned and to enjoy all the benefits that romance has to offer. Don't get tied up with rules and regulations that either don't apply to you or which are tedious.

14 SUNDAY *Moon Age Day 0 Moon Sign Aquarius*

This would be a good time for a brief withdrawal from some of the pressures of life, and this is a Sunday that offers the most if you spend it alongside family members, your partner or good friends. For the moment it's worth staying away from issues you find vexing, and leaving plans to mature at the back of your mind whilst you take a break.

15 MONDAY *Moon Age Day 1 Moon Sign Pisces*

A charming and easy-going manner is something that should come to you quite naturally under present planetary trends. You can use this to get more or less anything you want from others at this stage, though paradoxically your sensitivity to the needs and wants of those around you is not presently enhanced. All you require is balance.

16 TUESDAY *Moon Age Day 2 Moon Sign Pisces*

Domestic and family matters are once again brought back into the spotlight and there is now a special emphasis on property and possessions. Nostalgia could also play a significant role in your life around this time, but you need to bear in mind that some of the thoughts you have regarding the past are not realistic and may not represent what really happened.

17 WEDNESDAY *Moon Age Day 3 Moon Sign Aries*

The need to feel busy and useful is paramount, even if that means you decide to clear up after others and sort out situations that have nothing at all to do with you. Listening to what other people say is all very well, though remember that it may be out of kilter with what you know to be the truth. Biting your tongue would be no bad thing, at least for now.

18 THURSDAY *Moon Age Day 4 Moon Sign Aries*

There are signs that dealings with superiors or authority figures might prove to be a little awkward or troublesome during the last part of this working week, and you would be wise to be as patient as possible if you are to avoid losing your temper. It would be better by far to simply walk away from some issues rather than highlighting them.

19 FRIDAY *Moon Age Day 5 Moon Sign Aries*

Expectations are best kept to a minimum as you move towards this month's lunar low. For today at least you can still be quite positive in your approach, but you need to finish any jobs that are left undone and to clear the decks for actions that are going to take place next week. Stand by to deal with what could be a less than inspiring weekend.

20 SATURDAY *Moon Age Day 6 Moon Sign Taurus*

What you get from the lunar low this time around is very much down to the way you approach situations. It is important not to pit yourself against challenges that are never going to work out for you, no matter how much you try. Keep your expectations simple and enjoy what life offers quite naturally. If you are sensible, happiness should be possible.

21 SUNDAY *Moon Age Day 7 Moon Sign Taurus*

Beware of jumping to negative conclusions today, and rest easy in the knowledge that you can seek assistance if you need it. The lunar low demands a measured view of situations, and offers an interlude in which you can enjoy what your home life and personal relationships have to offer. This is not a good time for gambling or for taking chances.

22 MONDAY *Moon Age Day 8 Moon Sign Gemini*

You now have an opportunity to make life a whole lot more fulfilling, and to elicit strong emotional support both at home and when you are at work. If you are presently involved in full-time education, now is the time to push for significant progress, and affairs of the heart are positively highlighted for all Scorpios now.

23 TUESDAY *Moon Age Day 9 Moon Sign Gemini*

It's time to show your basic joy for life, and to use it to cheer up the most miserable people and to make the whole world smile along with you. This Scorpio should be a pleasure to have around, and you needn't go short of attention whilst the Sun remains in your solar fifth house. A far more flexible approach also becomes possible.

24 WEDNESDAY *Moon Age Day 10 Moon Sign Cancer*

Trends encourage a fascination for anything new or unusual as today unfolds. There is much to be said for leaving behind things you see as being outmoded or old fashioned, and this extends to the way you present yourself. If you know what looks right, be prepared to cut a dash in any kind of get-together, whether social or for business.

25 THURSDAY *Moon Age Day 11 Moon Sign Cancer*

When it comes to career developments it pays to be a self-starter and very energetic. For anyone to pull the wool over your eyes they would have to be extremely quick, particularly if you make sure your own mind is like lightning now. The only small problem at the moment could be if you decide to act first and ask questions later.

26 FRIDAY *Moon Age Day 12 Moon Sign Cancer*

Romantic affairs are positively highlighted, and getting your own way with others across the board is simply a matter of turning on the charm and asking for what you want in the right way. Who could refuse you? If ever there was a good time to try to get precisely what you want from the people around you, that time is today.

27 SATURDAY *Moon Age Day 13 Moon Sign Leo*

There could be scope for short cuts to success whilst the Moon moves through Leo. You have what it takes to impress authority figures, and to demonstrate exactly the right balance between being positive and also personally sensitive. In the main you can afford to help others out, no matter how strange the request might be.

28 SUNDAY *Moon Age Day 14 Moon Sign Leo*

There is a possibility you may decide to withdraw slightly on occasions today. You needn't allow this to interfere with your enjoyment of life at the moment because that remains strong. However, there are certain issues that are best dealt with through quiet thought, so removing yourself from the social maelstrom for brief periods is sensible.

March
2010

1 MONDAY *Moon Age Day 15 Moon Sign Virgo*

If you want to feel better about yourself and need assistance to safeguard your best interests, you could do worse than look to your romantic partner for support. Feelings of love and protection are available from a number of different directions, though you need to be careful that you don't end up feeling slightly suffocated by all this attention and care!

2 TUESDAY *Moon Age Day 16 Moon Sign Virgo*

You may well have to fall back on your own wits today, particularly if the standard way of doing things doesn't work too well. This means thinking on your feet, something you are very good at doing. There might not be much time today to take passengers on board, and if people can't keep up with your pace they could get left behind.

3 WEDNESDAY *Moon Age Day 17 Moon Sign Libra*

There could now be jobs to be done that you don't care for at all, and it would be extremely useful if you could somehow get others to do a few of them for you. Since your powers of persuasion are now well starred, you could make a virtue of fooling others into thinking you are doing them a favour when it is really the other way round.

4 THURSDAY *Moon Age Day 18 Moon Sign Libra*

A slightly quieter day is available ahead of the lunar high, and this particular Thursday should offer you the chance to sit and take stock much more than you have been able to do across the last week or so. By all means look to friends for impartial advice, but be slightly more wary of colleagues, some of whom may well have their own agenda.

5 FRIDAY *Moon Age Day 19 Moon Sign Scorpio*

This has potential to be a very good day when it comes to calling the shots, and you should use your present confidence to demonstrate to others that you can make the running. Your personal influence across the board should be there for all to see, and making things happen is the name of the game. The world can be your oyster now and across the weekend.

6 SATURDAY *Moon Age Day 20 Moon Sign Scorpio*

Even if some of your dreams are getting bigger all the time, there's nothing wrong with believing that a proportion of them could come true. If you can conceive it while the lunar high is present, you can probably also put it into action, which is why it is so important to remain positive. Good fortune is yours for the taking – so just take it!

7 SUNDAY *Moon Age Day 21 Moon Sign Sagittarius*

Although a slightly more reflective approach works well at the moment, there is still no reason why you should avoid either thinking big or putting plans into action. If you need assistance you should look for it nearby, though in the main you may be happy to go it alone. In matters of the heart it's a question of being dominant, but very attractive.

8 MONDAY *Moon Age Day 22 Moon Sign Sagittarius*

This is a time to be optimistic, cheerful and giving. The position of the Sun at the moment infers personal magnetism and great popularity among those with whom you live and work. You can use your charms to persuade others to do almost anything for you around now, so if there is any form of assistance you need, this is an ideal day to ask for it.

9 TUESDAY *Moon Age Day 23 Moon Sign Capricorn*

Communication, meeting people and getting on with what seems most important – that would be the perfect recipe for today. The really crucial thing is to get your ideas across in a way that enchants others and enthuses them to get on board with you. This is certainly no time to be a shrinking violet or to doubt your own abilities.

10 WEDNESDAY *Moon Age Day 24 Moon Sign Capricorn*

You should be in a position to achieve good results in a professional sense and to be quite certain of the steps you need to take in order to prosper. There is much to be said for looking after your money at this time and for not spending unnecessarily. However, if you are at the shops, by all means look out for a genuine bargain.

11 THURSDAY *Moon Age Day 25 Moon Sign Capricorn*

With the Sun still in your solar fifth house you have a chance to show the effervescent and creative side of your nature. Getting things looking right should be easier and you also have what it takes to please the sensitivities of those close to you. Romance is well highlighted and you can turn heads wherever you go at this stage of the month.

12 FRIDAY *Moon Age Day 26 Moon Sign Aquarius*

Could others describe you as being slightly overassertive at this time? The truth is that you know what you want from life, and it's natural to go around with all guns blazing in order to get it. Nevertheless, it's a good idea to show compassion, and Scorpio is rarely so selfish that it fails to notice the needs and wants of other people in the world.

13 SATURDAY *Moon Age Day 27 Moon Sign Aquarius*

You should be able to express yourself extremely well at this stage of the month, and that can be very important when it comes to scoring successes in life generally. Money matters can be sorted out, though it's worth keeping an eye on the spending tendencies of family members, particularly those who think your purse or wallet is bottomless.

14 SUNDAY *Moon Age Day 28 Moon Sign Pisces*

Your personality presently has great magnetism and impact – so much so that your popularity could be going off the scale. This gives you scope to increase your influence and to make the most of all the possibilities that are available to you on the social scene. This is one Sunday when you may decide you don't need much in the way of rest.

15 MONDAY *Moon Age Day 0 Moon Sign Pisces*

You have potential to be quite dramatic now, and in a way you may have lost your way because you could be on the stage! It's about being able to turn almost anything into a wonderful story, and that is one of the reasons why you can get on so well with others at this time. In a social sense you can demonstrate to others how eminently reasonable you are.

16 TUESDAY *Moon Age Day 1 Moon Sign Pisces*

Progress and advancement come under the spotlight at this time, though it is likely to be much more a case of doing what you do to the best of your ability rather than trying out too much that is completely new. You can afford to be proud of your recent actions, but don't let this get out of hand because there is probably more to do.

17 WEDNESDAY *Moon Age Day 2 Moon Sign Aries*

There is an emphasis is on your increasing self-confidence and this helps you to create a positive social scene. Complicated situations regarding friends are best avoided, as are disputes and arguments that have nothing to do with you. At home it's time to show how extremely kind and loving you can be, and people should appreciate these qualities in you.

18 THURSDAY *Moon Age Day 3 Moon Sign Aries*

When it comes to professional matters you need to weigh things in the balance today. The desire for fast results will not always be the best option and you can do a lot better today if you concentrate on one job at once. This would be an ideal time to slow things down somewhat, and this is down to the position of the Moon.

19 FRIDAY *Moon Age Day 4 Moon Sign Taurus*

Don't decide to do anything vital today and keep to tried and tested paths. The lunar low probably seems more severe if you have been moving along at a fast pace, and that could well have been the case for you. It's a little like having the brakes applied, and you will need to put in masses of extra effort today if you want to keep advancing.

20 SATURDAY *Moon Age Day 5 Moon Sign Taurus*

If energy is in short supply, the weekend may come as a welcome break from all the activity that has been surrounding you of late. Sharing fun and entertainment with family members is the order of the day, and it is in their direction that you are encouraged to turn at this time. Despite the lunar low, you should be happy to join in with the fun.

21 SUNDAY *Moon Age Day 6 Moon Sign Taurus*

The lunar low is still around during the first part of the day but you can ensure that the effect it has on you decreases as the hours advance. Today could be a good opportunity to do something different, and getting together with like-minded people to work for those who are less well off would be one option. Look for entertainment and diversion later.

22 MONDAY *Moon Age Day 7 Moon Sign Gemini*

Whilst the lunar low was upon you the Sun moved into your solar sixth house. Along comes a month-long spell during which you have scope to seek new accomplishments and finalise any details in your life that have been around for quite some time. A period of waiting is now at an end, and progress is there to be made.

23 TUESDAY *Moon Age Day 8 Moon Sign Gemini*

Venus is alongside your Sun and that assists you to get new incentives off to a good start today. There could not be a better time for getting involved in projects that really interest you, and you may even decide right now to turn a hobby into something much more. You needn't be quite as cautious at present as would often be the case.

24 WEDNESDAY *Moon Age Day 9 Moon Sign Cancer*

Does it appear that others are taking an opposite view to you today? A degree of patience is called for if you are not to lose your temper at some stage. You also need to be prepared to deal with a number of delays or cancellations, all of which could leave you feeling slightly frustrated and somewhat impotent in one way or another.

25 THURSDAY *Moon Age Day 10 Moon Sign Cancer*

Your skills could be in great demand at this stage of the month, especially where your working life is concerned. You can do things that others find extremely difficult, and a degree of showing off is only natural as a result. People shouldn't mind that, just as long as you can come up with the help they need at the most opportune time.

26 FRIDAY *Moon Age Day 11 Moon Sign Leo*

Your professional life would now benefit from a narrower focus and you can't afford to spread your talents about too much under present trends. It would be far better to do one thing properly than to undertake a wealth of tasks in a less than professional way. The end of this working week might also be an ideal time for a memorable social event.

27 SATURDAY *Moon Age Day 12 Moon Sign Leo*

Good results can be achieved through your practical efforts, even if you find it somewhat more difficult to put your thoughts into words. Explaining yourself fully could take time and might be a strain on your patience. Do you sometimes feel that you are surrounded by people who singularly fail to take any notice of what you are saying?

28 SUNDAY *Moon Age Day 13 Moon Sign Virgo*

Regular and social activities are what count today, and even if you are not doing much that is out of the ordinary, you have what it takes to turn mundane situations into little adventures. Why not do things in different ways and get others involved in your life to a greater extent? Romance also has much to offer you at this most fortunate time.

29 MONDAY *Moon Age Day 14 Moon Sign Virgo*

Avoid getting involved in any pushy activities at work. Your best approach is simply to keep everything you do visible and above board. If you act in a clandestine manner or decide to be subversive in some way you run a strong risk of getting yourself into trouble. There is an element of mischief about the present interlude.

30 TUESDAY *Moon Age Day 15 Moon Sign Libra*

The focus now turns in the direction of orderliness and efficiency. You probably find it difficult to understand people who are messy or unprepared, and you may decide to favour those who have a similar attitude to life. Today works best if you plan for the short term rather than looking too far ahead, and make the most of little opportunities that come your way.

31 WEDNESDAY *Moon Age Day 16 Moon Sign Libra*

If you feel your powers of influence are now slightly on the decline, there's nothing wrong with relying on the help of others. This sounds sensible, though it may not be very easy because you hate to feel reliant on anyone. There's also a danger of you becoming quite closed in your general attitude and retreating into yourself.

April

2010

1 THURSDAY *Moon Age Day 17 Moon Sign Scorpio*

The lunar high now emphasises the inspiring side of your nature as you enter the new month of April. There is nothing foolish about you, though you do have what it takes to make an April Fool out of just about anyone else. With a tremendous sense of fun you can use the lunar high to the best of your ability and make new friends on the way.

2 FRIDAY *Moon Age Day 18 Moon Sign Scorpio*

You can play an important role today by channelling your hopes and dreams into positive actions. You can also afford to take more chances than would normally be the case, and should be ready to throw in your lot with others in order to achieve a particular objective. In any group situation you can now put yourself in charge.

3 SATURDAY *Moon Age Day 19 Moon Sign Sagittarius*

Work and practical matters are still well accented, and the position of the Sun at this time is the reason. If fresh job offers are presented you should be quite willing to look at these in a positive way. There are gains to be made within personal relationships and once again the light of love should be in your eyes. Be available to help loved ones today.

4 SUNDAY *Moon Age Day 20 Moon Sign Sagittarius*

Now there is a real chance to improve your popularity rating, even among people you haven't always seen eye to eye with in the past. You can use your present communication skills to explain your motivations to others. If you're really successful in this task, they may be inclined to judge you less harshly in the future.

5 MONDAY *Moon Age Day 21 Moon Sign Sagittarius*

There could be less advantage available on the professional scene at the start of this month. Life has its complications, and you may well have to work extra hard in order to get the simplest things done. In a social sense you have scope for significantly more success, and you have what it takes to make new friends and influence people.

6 TUESDAY *Moon Age Day 22 Moon Sign Capricorn*

What a favourable period this can be for communications among your friends. It's worth making sure you are an important part of any new plans that are being laid down, and you might even decide to organise a journey you intend to make in the not too distant future. In a physical sense an active approach brings the best chance of winning.

7 WEDNESDAY *Moon Age Day 23 Moon Sign Capricorn*

Trends assist you to remain productive at work and to do especially well if you are involved in any sort of educational process at the moment. As usual for Scorpio, there is an emphasis on the delight you take in catering for the needs of others. This is especially the case for Scorpio people who are involved in the caring professions.

8 THURSDAY *Moon Age Day 24 Moon Sign Aquarius*

Make the most of what is going on as far as your domestic life is concerned, even if things are slowing down a little in other areas. It pays to keep abreast of local news and views at this time, and you may also decide to get involved in some sort of community project you see as being vitally important. This is a good time to plan ahead.

9 FRIDAY *Moon Age Day 25 Moon Sign Aquarius*

You could find yourself cast into opposing positions on a number of occasions today. One thing that is certain about Scorpio people is that they stick to their guns, and so you needn't feel obliged to change your mind about anything just to please the crowd. In the end it's a question of gaining the support of others by showing the strength of your convictions.

10 SATURDAY *Moon Age Day 26 Moon Sign Aquarius*

Bear in mind that the way you express yourself through words and actions could surprise some of the people around you. This is a weekend when you can shine socially and find enjoyment and reward in romance. If you have been looking for a new love, be prepared to focus your attention in a very specific direction now.

11 SUNDAY *Moon Age Day 27 Moon Sign Pisces*

You have what it takes to bring out the good side of all those you encounter today. It's natural to feel especially warm towards certain individuals, but this could also now extend to some you haven't cared for much in the past. Your communication skills are well marked at the moment and you can do yourself no end of good if you just keep on talking.

12 MONDAY *Moon Age Day 28 Moon Sign Pisces*

This would be a favourable time to throw in your lot with others in order to make better progress regarding a specific issue. It's true that you might not get all the glory if you have to share a success, but perhaps the end product makes this small sacrifice worthwhile. When it comes to looking after your finances a careful approach works best.

13 TUESDAY *Moon Age Day 29 Moon Sign Aries*

Practical matters are highlighted today and you need to be right on the ball when it comes to getting yourself organised. At the same time you are encouraged to look quite earnestly at the romantic side of your life and to invent new ways to pep things up a little. Use this period to move some of your more practical plans towards completion.

14 WEDNESDAY *Moon Age Day 0 Moon Sign Aries*

There are signs that your work circumstances at the moment could prove to be quite irritating, though if you are not in work or are retired, you have more scope to feel satisfied with your situation. All the same, this could be a difficult time to relax because the planets are encouraging you to burn off masses of energy.

15 THURSDAY *Moon Age Day 1 Moon Sign Taurus*

Stand by to deal with a few complications – that is, unless you are very organised. The lunar low encourages you to see things in a rather peculiar way and it may be difficult for you to find all the answers you seek until the weekend arrives. There is much to be said today for allowing colleagues and friends to take most of the strain.

16 FRIDAY *Moon Age Day 2 Moon Sign Taurus*

There could still be some setbacks to deal with, but as far as relationships are concerned you can ensure that everything is plain sailing. Realising this fact is part of the battle, and then it's a case of choosing to stay close to home whenever it proves to be possible. Something you are positively yearning for might just have to wait for a while.

17 SATURDAY *Moon Age Day 3 Moon Sign Taurus*

You can now happily seek out the support of family members and especially your partner. As the lunar low fades, a slightly more adventurous approach becomes possible, and you may decide you don't want to sit around at home during the weekend. The more competitive side of your nature is also emphasised now – so are you ready for some sport?

18 SUNDAY ☿ *Moon Age Day 4 Moon Sign Gemini*

Be prepared to deal with some unavoidable changes around now. Even if you don't welcome these at first, your strength lies in your willingness to adapt to altering circumstances. In a mental sense you can be on the ball and can use your quick mind to make short work of puzzles or downright mysteries.

19 MONDAY ☿ *Moon Age Day 5 Moon Sign Gemini*

You seem to have the secret of popularity at the start of this week and you should be able to get things working in the way you want by simply being your present charming self. Part of this task is persuading people to put themselves out on your behalf, and for some of them it's a case of repaying debts from the past that they feel are owed.

20 TUESDAY ☿ *Moon Age Day 6 Moon Sign Cancer*

Things taking place at work, or within social groups of which you are a part, make it possible for you to be progressive and even excited at prospects that stand before you. There is something unusual about your nature at this time, and you have everything you need to show how extremely innovative and even pioneering you can be in a number of ways.

21 WEDNESDAY ☿ *Moon Age Day 7 Moon Sign Cancer*

In love relationships you should now be motivated to create a warm and pleasant atmosphere. This helps you to increase your popularity no end and to revitalise any one-to-one encounters that have been flagging somewhat recently. There may be some slight difficulties in terms of arrangements, but these can be overcome.

22 THURSDAY ☿ *Moon Age Day 8 Moon Sign Leo*

The greatest rewards are still likely to come from personal relationships and fortunate encounters with people to whom you are attracted. Don't be surprised if you are able to elicit compliments today from rather unexpected directions. After all, you have what it takes to become flavour of the month with at least one very surprising individual.

23 FRIDAY ☿ *Moon Age Day 9 Moon Sign Leo*

You might be tempted to ignore some of the important details of life today, and if so, you could well be slapped in the face by a few mishaps. It would be better to proceed cautiously and to check and double-check details at this time. In the financial sphere it also pays to be fanatical about getting things right.

24 SATURDAY ☿ *Moon Age Day 10 Moon Sign Virgo*

All group encounters offer the chance to make progress, and this is a time when you should be quite happy to co-operate fully with others. Maybe this is friends or even colleagues if you work at the weekend, but whatever the circumstances might be, you can now afford to forego your own personal opinions for the sake of cordiality.

25 SUNDAY ☿ *Moon Age Day 11 Moon Sign Virgo*

Personal relationships maintain their importance to you now, and this is a day when you can find both the time and the incentive to show someone just how much you care for them. Feeling more at one with the world as a whole counts for a great deal now, and assists you to get on well with just about anyone you encounter.

26 MONDAY ☿ *Moon Age Day 12 Moon Sign Libra*

Real fulfilment today is possible when you give up all thought of making a good solo impression and throw in your lot with those around you. The greater the co-operation, the better the results, and you can feel warm inside at the thought of your contribution to communal efforts. Under all the activity, a contemplative approach is still worth pursuing.

27 TUESDAY ☿ *Moon Age Day 13 Moon Sign Libra*

Present planetary trends encourage a desire to be liked by others, and you may be willing to go to previously unexpected lengths to make sure this is the case. The spotlight is now on friends and on the firm support and good ideas you can gain from them. At home you are in a position to take a very understanding view.

28 WEDNESDAY ☿ *Moon Age Day 14 Moon Sign Scorpio*

Now is the time to take many of your previous plans and make them into realities. There are gains available that you may not have foreseen, though some of these are probably as a result of your previous efforts. Good luck is there for the taking, and this is a period during which you can afford to take more chances than usual.

29 THURSDAY ☿ *Moon Age Day 15 Moon Sign Scorpio*

The lunar high is an ideal chance to put fresh ideas to the test and make suggestions to see how others are likely to react. Your powers of persuasion are now enhanced, and it shouldn't be hard for you to get your own way, often without others realising that it is happening. A day to bring as much change into your life as you can and to travel around whenever possible.

30 FRIDAY ☿ *Moon Age Day 16 Moon Sign Scorpio*

Security becomes a key issue, but in a very positive way. There are good ideas on offer all the time, and you needn't be tardy when it comes to trying out a few of them in the real world. There is much more emphasis on the practical than on the theory while the Moon maintains its present position, and your good cheer should be there for all to see.

May

2010

1 SATURDAY ☿ *Moon Age Day 17 Moon Sign Sagittarius*

Do avoid getting on the wrong side of people who you see as authority figures. It's not that you can't disagree with them, but that you may worry and fret about the situation later. There is no reason to fall out with anyone at this time, that is, unless you allow the really stubborn side of your nature to predominate.

2 SUNDAY ☿ *Moon Age Day 18 Moon Sign Sagittarius*

You could do worse than to involve yourself in twosomes today, and this applies even beyond the scope of romantic attachments. More progress is possible when you are alongside someone you like, and the sum of the whole is almost certain to be greater than the parts. You may well be able to attract some backhanded compliments around now.

3 MONDAY ☿ *Moon Age Day 19 Moon Sign Capricorn*

There is much to be said for seeking advice from folks you meet around this time and for listening carefully to what they are saying. Taken together with your own slant on life, their considerations can help you make a greater success of present efforts. This is certainly no time to go it alone or to be churlish about co-operation.

4 TUESDAY ☿ *Moon Age Day 20 Moon Sign Capricorn*

With Venus in your solar eighth house now your sensitivity is heightened and you should listen to that little voice at the back of your mind that offers you the most sensible advice. Trends suggest you could be somewhat foolish regarding love, or it may be that you are accepting some sort of treatment that you would normally refuse altogether.

5 WEDNESDAY ☿ *Moon Age Day 21 Moon Sign Aquarius*

It's important to be fully abreast of all that is taking place in the world around you and to ensure that very little escapes your scrutiny now. If you remain on the ball you shouldn't be easily fooled. However, the same may not be the case for your friends, and it's worth being ready to offer them your wise counsel and sound advice at this time.

6 THURSDAY ☿ *Moon Age Day 22 Moon Sign Aquarius*

The Moon briefly enters your solar fourth house, offering a slightly quieter spell across the next couple of days. A more contemplative interlude becomes possible in which you may be quite happy to spend protracted periods on your own. Fortunately there are strong social impulses around too, encouraging a chattier approach when you are with others.

7 FRIDAY ☿ *Moon Age Day 23 Moon Sign Aquarius*

Look for opportunities to create a special time with someone you love and make this a day for showing how deep your affections run. In the midst of a busy life it is sometimes difficult to find the time you need to say the right things and to offer undying support, but that needn't be the case around now. It's a question of proving your devotion.

8 SATURDAY ☿ *Moon Age Day 24 Moon Sign Pisces*

Greater self-awareness and the ability to express yourself positively are gifts coming from the Moon this weekend. You have improved creative potential and plenty of desire to make your home circumstances better and more comfortable. This doesn't mean you have to stick closely to your own abode, because travel is also part of the planetary possibilities.

9 SUNDAY ☿ *Moon Age Day 25 Moon Sign Pisces*

An ideal day for intimacy and for making a big fuss of your partner. This is the person you rely on the most and they deserve your unswerving loyalty and assistance when it is needed. Outside of romance, the time is right to make important new friends, and you might even meet someone you wish you had known for longer. A smile can work wonders.

10 MONDAY ☿ *Moon Age Day 26 Moon Sign Aries*

There is much to be said for keeping busy for most of today, particularly if there is plenty to do and you are keen to get it all done at the same time. It's possible that practical commitments will outweigh your own wishes for the moment, and you may not be able to find much time to simply enjoy yourself alongside your friends.

11 TUESDAY ☿ *Moon Age Day 27 Moon Sign Aries*

You should be feeling very warm and affectionate whilst the Sun is in your solar seventh house, and you can use this interlude to make the most of romantic gestures. Whether all of these come from an expected or even an acceptable direction remains to be seen, but you can afford to be quite flattered in any case by the attention.

12 WEDNESDAY ☿ *Moon Age Day 28 Moon Sign Aries*

Do try to avoid obstacles and difficult situations today. The best way to achieve this is to stick to what you know well and to stay away from jobs that look awkward from the start. There are times when it is fortunate and even desirable to pit your wits against life, but for the moment you need to be comfortable with what you are doing.

13 THURSDAY *Moon Age Day 29 Moon Sign Taurus*

There is a slight chance you will feel somewhat alone and probably slightly confused whilst the lunar low is present this month. Does it seem more difficult to get the support you feel you need? If you look at situations without emotion you might see that nothing is expected of you that you haven't done a thousand times before.

14 FRIDAY *Moon Age Day 0 Moon Sign Taurus*

Taking risks is probably not a sensible option for today at least. Once again it is important to stick to what you know and understand, whilst staying away from anything that might get you into trouble or which could prove physically dangerous. Safety and security are your keywords, and you may well find these qualities within your home.

15 SATURDAY *Moon Age Day 1 Moon Sign Gemini*

If you are looking for new friends at this time, why not look for people who can help you to bring out new sides to your nature or who cultivate your more refined qualities? Just at present the more educated and sensible aspects of your character are emphasised, assisting you to attract a 'certain' sort of person. You needn't forget old friends, though.

16 SUNDAY *Moon Age Day 2 Moon Sign Gemini*

This should be a wonderful time for creating intimate encounters and for strengthening the ties between yourself and your loved one. If you don't have a life partner and wish you did, this would be an ideal interlude to look around. Things are more likely to come your way if you put in the right sort of effort at an opportune moment.

17 MONDAY *Moon Age Day 3 Moon Sign Cancer*

There is good scope for cultivating your social life, and the start of this week also coincides with a period during which you have what it takes to get your own way for most of the time. It's a question of persuading people to follow your lead and to do what they can to make you feel secure and happy. Look after money and avoid being spendthrift.

18 TUESDAY *Moon Age Day 4 Moon Sign Cancer*

This would be a wonderful day to seek wide open spaces and to make the most of the natural world that surrounds you. With the early summer comes a greater desire to encounter nature in all its variety, and there is an emphasis on spending plenty of time out of doors. This would also be a great time for thinking about taking an early vacation.

19 WEDNESDAY *Moon Age Day 5 Moon Sign Leo*

Trends encourage you to feel good about yourself at the moment, though in a fairly quiet sort of way. There's a confidence about you that you should be happy to display to others, and this helps you to gain the backing you need for your ideas. Remember that humour is important in relationships, and that entertaining others can really make a difference.

20 THURSDAY *Moon Age Day 6 Moon Sign Leo*

Some key aims and objectives are due for an overhaul, and this would be a favourable time to put your mind to the test. It's possible that not everything will go your way first time, and there is merit in trying again if anything does go wrong. As far as using your time is concerned, try to strike a sensible balance between work and home.

21 FRIDAY *Moon Age Day 7 Moon Sign Virgo*

Join forces with friends in order to get the most from situations. This is not the best time for going it alone, and in any case you can make sure there is much more entertainment when you co-operate. It's worth bearing in mind that you can't be flavour of the month for everyone.

22 SATURDAY *Moon Age Day 8 Moon Sign Virgo*

Chats and even debates with others can offer you scope for inspiration and might be the source of many new ideas. Your innovative qualities are presently to the fore, and you have what it takes to be out there and succeeding for most of the time. Keep a sense of proportion when it comes to financial issues, and don't spend what you don't have.

23 SUNDAY *Moon Age Day 9 Moon Sign Virgo*

Be prepared to eliminate old convictions and turn your mind to the future with less inclination to hang onto the past. Scorpio is famous for maintaining a way of being that is sometimes distinctly old fashioned, but you needn't take this approach under present trends. On the contrary, you can afford to be about as contemporary as it is possible to be.

24 MONDAY *Moon Age Day 10 Moon Sign Libra*

Mars is now in your solar tenth house and this encourages you to take note of new initiatives, while still sticking to tried and tested paths. Deciding not to opt for change for its own sake is all very well, but that doesn't mean you should go back to being stuck in the past. Some situations can be confusing, but humour should help you through.

25 TUESDAY *Moon Age Day 11 Moon Sign Libra*

You can see things changing around you all the time and sometimes this might make you feel less than secure. With the Moon in its present position there is much to be said for finding comfort at home, but as the hours advance you can allow your curiosity to bring you out into the world. By the evening you should be set to have a good time.

26 WEDNESDAY *Moon Age Day 12 Moon Sign Scorpio*

There is genuine power available at your fingertips and you can use it to have a go at almost anything now that the lunar high has arrived. This is the time of the month to throw caution to the wind and to go out and get what you want the most. Getting others to follow your lead should be within your abilities, and the admirers could well be gathering!

27 THURSDAY *Moon Age Day 13 Moon Sign Scorpio*

Energy is boosted and your level of good luck is also enhanced. This would be a great day for a shopping spree or for doing something completely different alongside those you find stimulating and fascinating. If you decide to cross swords with anyone at the moment, you stand a good chance of winning the argument with little effort.

28 FRIDAY *Moon Age Day 14 Moon Sign Sagittarius*

Pleasure can now be gained from all sorts of journeys or from ringing the changes as far as your home life is concerned. A more independent attitude prevails, and you needn't rely on others to make necessary arrangements. Energy levels are off the scale, and although the lunar high has passed you should still be motoring at a great speed.

29 SATURDAY *Moon Age Day 15 Moon Sign Sagittarius*

Strength of will is one of your greatest virtues, as is the ability to keep going when others have fallen by the wayside. Today is about not only sorting out your own life but also spending time making sure that everyone else is getting the success they desire. In reality it might be easier to help others now than to help yourself.

30 SUNDAY *Moon Age Day 16 Moon Sign Capricorn*

You have an opportunity to make lots of interesting things happen this weekend and you shouldn't be short of something to think about. If you are involved in practical jobs you should be showing just how accurate you are capable of being. Ask yourself whether it's worth getting hung up on details. Better by far to look towards general progress.

31 MONDAY *Moon Age Day 17 Moon Sign Capricorn*

Seeking advice from someone who is older or wiser than you are would be no bad thing, and when it comes to specific tasks you might decide to call on the support of professionals. Your home environment can offer you the support you need, and you can make the most of all the positive influences you gain from friends.

June 2010

1 TUESDAY *Moon Age Day 18 Moon Sign Capricorn*

Beware of getting bogged down with details. This could be something of an issue under present trends, and your best approach is to aim at particular objectives without worrying too much about the specific actions you will need to take. It pays to split situations up into different tasks and deal with these one at a time.

2 WEDNESDAY *Moon Age Day 19 Moon Sign Aquarius*

When it comes to professional matters a more rugged approach is the order of the day, and you probably won't suffer fools gladly. By all means do what you can for people who are willing to help themselves, though giving constant assistance when you know it is wasted is another matter. Get ready to create a positive social evening.

3 THURSDAY *Moon Age Day 20 Moon Sign Aquarius*

Mercury has now moved into your solar seventh house and that supports a rather breezy phase in your life in which you have scope to open new avenues of communication. Getting on with people who have been difficult in the past could be one option, though there's nothing wrong with being selective about who you choose to help.

4 FRIDAY *Moon Age Day 21 Moon Sign Pisces*

The time is right to think hard about getting rid of anything that is proving to be a trial. In extreme cases this could be a relationship that has definitely run its course, though you might still continue to be ruled to a great extent by nostalgia. Be consistent in your dealings with family members at this time.

5 SATURDAY *Moon Age Day 22 Moon Sign Pisces*

A more romantic view of life is on offer with the Moon in its present position. This could assist you to create a warm and comfortable sort of weekend, though you may still be plagued by dreams of adventures you are not pursuing at the moment. There is a sort of dissatisfaction within you that needs addressing.

6 SUNDAY *Moon Age Day 23 Moon Sign Pisces*

Some conflicts are possible whilst Mars occupies your solar tenth house, though these are likely to be professional rather than personal so they may not be evident on a Sunday. It's fine to communicate with someone you haven't seen for quite some time, though you need to consider whether you really wish to open up certain aspects of the past.

7 MONDAY *Moon Age Day 24 Moon Sign Aries*

Trends assist you to be very focused at the present time, so if there is anything you need to organise this is clearly the best time to do it. It's worth keeping career goals uppermost in your mind, and using your current abilities to carry other people along with you when it comes to even audacious plans. You could be on top form physically.

8 TUESDAY *Moon Age Day 25 Moon Sign Aries*

Are things a little tense at the moment? This is related to the presence of Mars in your solar eleventh house. Flare-ups are possible when it comes to social attachments, but you can take steps to ensure that it is less likely in the case of really close friends. Part of the trouble is your current inclination to speak your mind, no matter what.

9 WEDNESDAY *Moon Age Day 26 Moon Sign Taurus*

You have scope to quieten things down whilst the lunar low is in evidence. This period should at least give you the chance to formalise your plans for the future, and you needn't allow yourself to be bothered by outside influences to the extent that has been the case recently. Withdrawing into your own little world does have its own advantages.

10 THURSDAY *Moon Age Day 27 Moon Sign Taurus*

This is definitely the right time of the month to recharge your batteries. Let others do things for you and don't be too worried if some jobs are being put on hold. You shouldn't feel too anxious about responsibilities, particularly if in most respects you are well on top of things. Taking a break is the order of the day.

11 FRIDAY *Moon Age Day 28 Moon Sign Gemini*

In joint monetary affairs you need to make the most of the good luck that is now available. Co-operation now seems to be the key to success, and there is much to be said for throwing in your lot with people who clearly know where they are going. There could still be the odd delay or difficulty, but nothing you can't deal with.

12 SATURDAY *Moon Age Day 0 Moon Sign Gemini*

Personal relationships could be very supportive, and you shouldn't have any difficulty finding the right words to please those who are important to you. On the contrary, you can become a veritable poet at this time, and with the present position of little Mercury offering so much support you could be making new friends simply by saying the right thing.

13 SUNDAY *Moon Age Day 1 Moon Sign Gemini*

Travel could now be uppermost in your mind, and it looks as though Scorpio may be getting itchy feet. Taking journeys in your own locality would be no bad thing, but for a few lucky individuals the world beckons. What is most important around now is to avoid getting stuck in any sort of rut, either socially or with regard to your home life.

14 MONDAY *Moon Age Day 2 Moon Sign Cancer*

You can now have a very positive influence over others, and joint finances especially are well highlighted under present planetary trends. If you have been in any doubt about any sort of investment, you now have the ability to find the answers you need. It's all very well putting certain things on ice for a while, but now is the time to move.

15 TUESDAY *Moon Age Day 3 Moon Sign Cancer*

A day to capitalise on new opportunities in the professional world. Some Scorpio subjects will be in a position to seek out greater responsibility but also better financial remuneration. It pays to look after your personal resources very carefully, and not to spend too much on unnecessary luxuries.

16 WEDNESDAY *Moon Age Day 4 Moon Sign Leo*

You needn't allow yourself to get involved in pointless arguments just because you feel you have to be in the right. Ask yourself whether it really matters, particularly if those who are opposed to you are never going to accept your point of view. Your best approach is to say what you must and then leave it alone. Instead of arguing, why not enjoy yourself?

17 THURSDAY *Moon Age Day 5 Moon Sign Leo*

Remember that you cannot please all of the people all of the time, and it might not even be worth trying to do so today. There are always going to be individuals who know their own mind best, and you need to get used to that fact. It's a question of getting on with what matters to you, even if in some cases you feel it is necessary to go it alone.

18 FRIDAY *Moon Age Day 6 Moon Sign Virgo*

An ability to win the confidence of your friends is inherent in your nature, but if there are a lot of awkward people around at the moment that could be quite difficult to do. Be prepared to review today's tasks and decide whether you can afford to slacken your pace. Strong social inclinations are a natural part of life now.

19 SATURDAY *Moon Age Day 7 Moon Sign Virgo*

You have what it takes to make exciting things happen around you today, especially in terms of friendship, and you might even be tempted to indulge in a little public speaking. The artistic side of your nature is also emphasised this weekend, encouraging you to do what you can to spruce up your home surroundings.

20 SUNDAY *Moon Age Day 8 Moon Sign Libra*

By all means remain contemplative, but at the same time be aware of opportunities to make a good impression on the right people. This could be almost anyone, from a really important authority figure to a tramp you see in the street. Class or standing doesn't really come into it today, because you should be interested in everyone.

21 MONDAY *Moon Age Day 9 Moon Sign Libra*

You should be able to make this a fairly successful sort of day, particularly if you are organised and you know what you want from life. Remember that this may not be true of those around you, and in the case of family members especially you need to be prepared to make decisions if your nearest and dearest are unwilling to do so.

22 TUESDAY *Moon Age Day 10 Moon Sign Scorpio*

Individual success is now very important to you, and with the lunar high paying a visit you will have what it takes to keep a very high profile and to impress people with your sound reasoning. You can also take advantage of the luck that is available under this influence of the Moon, and focusing your efforts in the direction of money would be no bad thing.

23 WEDNESDAY *Moon Age Day 11 Moon Sign Scorpio*

Your thirst for life is highlighted under this influence and you should be using your creative talents to the full. This would be an excellent time to go travelling, whether or not you have arranged a journey in advance. Fresh fields and pastures new count for a great deal now, and you need to let the power of the summer have an influence on you.

24 THURSDAY *Moon Age Day 12 Moon Sign Sagittarius*

At work you have the ability to create a good impression. This can be quite important because there are gains to be made and people to influence. This word 'influence' is very important to Scorpio this year, and especially so at this time. It's a case of realising that life is not a rehearsal and doing all you can to get to the winning post early.

25 FRIDAY *Moon Age Day 13 Moon Sign Sagittarius*

Strong emotions are evident, encouraging you not to be tardy when it comes to telling people what you think. In romantic situations you can find the right words to knock people for six, and can use the sheer power of your personality in just about any circumstances. Is it worth worrying about the few people who don't really like you?

26 SATURDAY *Moon Age Day 14 Moon Sign Sagittarius*

A day to exercise your freedom to go out and make discoveries – things that are going to be of importance to you in the weeks and months ahead. By ensuring you have a better understanding of what is needed in any given situation you can impress the right people, and should be able to create a weekend to remember!

27 SUNDAY *Moon Age Day 15 Moon Sign Capricorn*

Your greatest benefits today come from being in the right place at the best possible time, and in order to know where this might be on any given occasion you need to use your very strong intuition. When that little voice at the back of your mind tells you to take a specific course of action, rather than arguing with it, your best response is simply to comply.

28 MONDAY *Moon Age Day 16 Moon Sign Capricorn*

Independence is valued highly by Scorpio at the best of times, but proves to be extremely important under present trends. You probably won't take at all kindly to being told what to do by people you don't admire, and if you are put into uncomfortable situations you can certainly afford to speak out.

29 TUESDAY *Moon Age Day 17 Moon Sign Aquarius*

It's worth bringing new ideas and philosophies into your life whilst Mercury occupies its present position in your solar chart. Trends support an attraction to unusual things and to people who are definitely not run of the mill. It is through other people that you can make your most important discoveries, and your sociable nature is of great importance now.

30 WEDNESDAY *Moon Age Day 18 Moon Sign Aquarius*

A greater sense of freedom is now on offer, and you really do need to look at the world in more detail – which could well mean travel. If you have a holiday planned for this period you have chosen wisely, but even if you can only find the time to go to the shops or the local park, you still have an opportunity to learn something of importance.

July 2010

1 THURSDAY *Moon Age Day 19 Moon Sign Aquarius*

Relating to others proves to be extremely important at the start of July and you can learn a great deal by listening to what is being said around you. Almost anything can assist you to develop new ideas, and there are good reasons to join in with potentially exciting possibilities. Scorpio is sometimes fairly reserved, but that needn't be the case at present.

2 FRIDAY *Moon Age Day 20 Moon Sign Pisces*

An ideal day to get yourself in the mood for romance and to use what you learn from others to turn yourself into the perfect suitor. Don't be afraid to let your light shine in social situations, and be prepared to be the life and soul of any party that is taking place. If there isn't one in the offing, one option is to arrange it yourself!

3 SATURDAY *Moon Age Day 21 Moon Sign Pisces*

There are gains to be made by focusing on monetary or personal situations today and by making sure everything is in the right place at home. Bear in mind that any disorganisation now could lead to minor frustrations further down the road. Give and take are important components in personal relationships, a fact you should not forget.

4 SUNDAY *Moon Age Day 22 Moon Sign Aries*

Keep your eyes and ears open for new input at this time and enjoy the cut and thrust of a fairly hectic life. Today offers an opportunity to get ahead of yourself by doing tasks that don't really need to be completed for a while, and by doing a little extra at home in order to free yourself from routines in the days that lie ahead of you.

5 MONDAY *Moon Age Day 23 Moon Sign Aries*

Bustling activity is the order of the day, and you may well decide to spend more time out of doors than would normally be the case. For younger Scorpios in particular, this would be an ideal period for sleeping out under the stars – or at least staying up late. The night time is always important to your zodiac sign, but rarely so much as it proves to be now.

6 TUESDAY *Moon Age Day 24 Moon Sign Aries*

Today is all about ingenuity and being in the right place to benefit from a host of new possibilities that presently surround you. Activities of all kinds should help you to feel vital and alive, and this could prove to be extremely significant in the longer term. Bear in mind who is watching you just now. Could they single you out for special treatment later?

7 WEDNESDAY *Moon Age Day 25 Moon Sign Taurus*

With the lunar low comes the possibility of a slightly quieter phase, but that does at least give you the chance to look at things more deeply. Even if you are less inclined to get involved in things for the next couple of days, it's still worth watching. A little break should offer you the time to come up with new ideas and altered strategies.

8 THURSDAY *Moon Age Day 26 Moon Sign Taurus*

Getting your own way with others could now be a whole lot more difficult than it seemed to be even a couple of days ago. Rather than persisting, why not allow the water of life to flow over and around you for a few hours? If you relax and enjoy what is taking place, the lunar low can prove to be a very useful and productive time.

9 FRIDAY *Moon Age Day 27 Moon Sign Gemini*

Enhancing career ambitions now becomes possible, particularly if you are determined to shake off the negative effects of the lunar low. It might take a while for you to get going at the start of today, but once you get yourself in gear there should be no stopping you. If you show others you are being positive, you can persuade them to get involved.

10 SATURDAY *Moon Age Day 28 Moon Sign Gemini*

There's a danger of your being slightly overbearing in discussions, a legacy of an eleventh-house Mars, but at least you can leave others in no doubt as to what you want. If you take the right approach you can avoid arguments, even if others think you are a little too bossy at the moment. The end doesn't always justify the means, so tread carefully today.

11 SUNDAY *Moon Age Day 29 Moon Sign Cancer*

It's time for a complete change of scenery and for a short break, so taking on too much in the way of routine chores wouldn't be sensible today. Better by far to keep a few hours free to accompany your partner, family members or friends on some sort of outing, and to go somewhere that stimulates your mental faculties as well as offering physical exercise.

12 MONDAY *Moon Age Day 0 Moon Sign Cancer*

Travel plans are well accented at the moment, and no matter what sort of journey you are planning, you should be in a position to have a good time. Today works best if you try to arrange things so that you can take some time out to enjoy yourself, and don't allow yourself to be so busy that you fail to have a minute to spare.

13 TUESDAY *Moon Age Day 1 Moon Sign Leo*

Trends encourage you to keep professional issues uppermost in your mind and to make the most of some very progressive influences that are available around now. Any new information that you obtain needs to be thought about carefully because it is likely you can do yourself some good by a simple change of tack.

14 WEDNESDAY *Moon Age Day 2 Moon Sign Leo*

There is much to be said for taking a day off to go exploring, or at the very least spending a few hours in the company of someone you really like. It's time to have fun, and you won't get much of that if you follow the same old workday routines. Anything old, unusual or just plain different has potential to fascinate you now.

15 THURSDAY *Moon Age Day 3 Moon Sign Virgo*

An ideal day to cultivate the warmth and security that comes with friendship and to allow the romantic side of your nature to show more. Twosomes are favoured under present trends, and you may discover something to your advantage from within a fond embrace. Rather than getting hung up on details at work, try to look at the bigger picture.

16 FRIDAY *Moon Age Day 4 Moon Sign Virgo*

Around this time you may have to reassess the effect you have on other people, particularly if you feel that in some cases recently it hasn't been as positive as you would have wished. When it comes to teamwork issues the emphasis is on being totally honest with yourself and on starting to do things in a quite different way.

17 SATURDAY *Moon Age Day 5 Moon Sign Libra*

Trends at this time favour long journeys and cultural interests. If you can get away from your usual duties and responsibilities, now would be a good time to do so. New experiences can be integrated into your life, and the simple act of being away from your routines, even for a short while, can prove to be very useful.

18 SUNDAY *Moon Age Day 6 Moon Sign Libra*

This is not a good day to believe everything you hear. It's worth reassessing recent projects you thought were fully sorted and deciding whether you need to go back to the drawing board and start again. Life can be quite a roller coaster, but you can make sure that it is also very interesting. Seeking help from friends would be no bad thing.

19 MONDAY *Moon Age Day 7 Moon Sign Scorpio*

You can now take advantage of enhanced energy levels, and for that you can thank the lunar high. Burning the candle at both ends becomes a real possibility, and you shouldn't be in the least fazed if you have to work long and hard in order to achieve your objectives. You also have scope to mix work with fun at this most interesting time.

20 TUESDAY *Moon Age Day 8 Moon Sign Scorpio*

You should be able to tap into more than a little good luck at the moment, and some of the benefits you gain come from quite unexpected directions. It's time to take your hunches and use them to your advantage, also drawing on that almost psychic quality you possess. Money could be easier to make now, but it's also much easier to spend!

21 WEDNESDAY *Moon Age Day 9 Moon Sign Sagittarius*

This is a period of expanding interests and total concentration on specific issues. That doesn't mean you can't enjoy yourself too. On the contrary, you should know instinctively how to compartment your life in order to get the best from every situation. It's worth taking a little rest at the end of the day if you are running out of steam.

22 THURSDAY *Moon Age Day 10 Moon Sign Sagittarius*

Planetary trends now favour issues associated with finance and the practical world around you. If there are contracts to sign or new plans to put into action, this is an ideal time to address such matters. In a social sense today is positive for getting on well with new friends and for meeting people once more that you haven't seen for years.

23 FRIDAY *Moon Age Day 11 Moon Sign Sagittarius*

You never know what you might learn, and just at the moment you should be fully open to all manner of new possibilities. That's why it is vitally important to keep your ears and eyes wide open and to be involved in as many conversations as proves to be possible. Even apparent gossip shouldn't be beyond your interest at the moment.

24 SATURDAY *Moon Age Day 12 Moon Sign Capricorn*

Career considerations come under the spotlight, even though the weekend has arrived. If you can't actively alter your working circumstances today, you should at least be in a good position to plan for next week. At the same time the social impulses within you are still highlighted, encouraging you to seek out the company of interesting people.

25 SUNDAY *Moon Age Day 13 Moon Sign Capricorn*

Make sure you are fully aware of interesting things that are taking place around you at the present time. With everything to play for in the romantic stakes you have a chance to make the best possible impression on your partner – or someone you wish was your partner. In terms of family attachments, feelings of love and security are the order of the day.

26 MONDAY *Moon Age Day 14 Moon Sign Aquarius*

Recent demands on your time could well slacken somewhat under present trends, and with the Moon in your solar fourth house for the next couple of days there are good reasons to focus a great percentage of your efforts and energy on your home and family. Don't forget to make time for fairly routine but nevertheless important discussions.

27 TUESDAY *Moon Age Day 15 Moon Sign Aquarius*

Career matters could now have more going for them than might have been the case yesterday, but it's still important for you to look towards your home for happiness and reassurance. Any slight feelings of insecurity at the moment are best dealt with by seeking out family members.

28 WEDNESDAY *Moon Age Day 16 Moon Sign Aquarius*

There are signs that your strong opinions won't appeal to everyone today, and you may need to tone down your beliefs somewhat if you are not to offer some unintended offence. In group situations you might not be quite as adept as you were a few weeks ago, but with a little effort on your part you can still win through and gain people's confidence.

29 THURSDAY *Moon Age Day 17 Moon Sign Pisces*

Look out for a new phase of major developments regarding your career, as well as new opportunities to make progress in group-based social projects. You tend to be quite practical at the best of times, but might be especially so with the Sun in your solar tenth house. Kindness towards a friend can really make a difference now.

30 FRIDAY *Moon Age Day 18 Moon Sign Pisces*

Romantic matters are now positively underlined, and there is much to be said for looking and feeling at your best. With everything to play for in a social sense you have scope to make a good impression on the world at large and can get a great deal out of even apparently random meetings. Don't underestimate your own present abilities.

31 SATURDAY *Moon Age Day 19 Moon Sign Aries*

There are enhancements to your social life available around now, and spending time out of doors is also well accented. The alfresco life can be wonderful at this point in the year, and this would also be an ideal time for making changes to your domestic surroundings, or even more likely your garden.

August

2010

1 SUNDAY

Moon Age Day 20 Moon Sign Aries

You should be able to take advantage of plenty of support around now, and some of it may be from quite unlikely directions. Ask yourself whether it is actually all that surprising, particularly if what is happening is that people you have helped in the past are now returning the favour. A potentially active phase assists you to enliven your life no end.

2 MONDAY

Moon Age Day 21 Moon Sign Aries

Don't leave anything to chance today. With an opportunity for a couple of quieter days coming up, it would be sensible to make sure that all loose ends are tied up right now. You should still be able to mix and mingle, though there's nothing wrong with leaving some slack in your social calendar between now and later on in the week.

3 TUESDAY

Moon Age Day 22 Moon Sign Taurus

The lunar low is a time to pace yourself and to avoid taking on so much that you become fatigued by it all. 'One thing at once' seems to be the best adage for you, and you would be well advised to leave any really arduous tasks until a later date. Remember that what others are up to right now is probably not your concern, so curb your curiosity.

4 WEDNESDAY

Moon Age Day 23 Moon Sign Taurus

You may now decide that some plans need to be totally abandoned or at the very least postponed until a more sensible time. You can afford to let others do things for you, because relationships are a two-way street and people often want to help you out. This is not a day to be too proud or to turn down the chance to be spoiled in some way.

5 THURSDAY *Moon Age Day 24 Moon Sign Gemini*

Mars is now in your solar twelfth house, indicating that life goes most smoothly for you when you bear other people's needs and wants in mind. Fortunately this is part of your basic nature so you should be well in tune with what is happening astrologically. You have everything you need now to steer those around you towards compromises.

6 FRIDAY *Moon Age Day 25 Moon Sign Gemini*

Be prepared to project yourself as much as possible today and to take on any new responsibilities that interest you. If you feel you are not working to your full potential at the present time, ask yourself whether you could do more to promote your own interests. Unusual or surprising responses work best if you are dealing with original sorts of people.

7 SATURDAY *Moon Age Day 26 Moon Sign Cancer*

Right now your social motivations are emphasised, and there are gains to be made from working in groups. Even if the thought of going it alone is appealing, it is less likely to get you the accolades than if you get involved with others. Some patience is necessary because you don't suffer fools gladly, and there could now be one or two around.

8 SUNDAY *Moon Age Day 27 Moon Sign Cancer*

This is a time when you should be setting out to improve your mind as much as possible. The more you stretch yourself, the greater are likely to be the ultimate rewards. Any sort of puzzle could have a particular fascination for you under present trends, and you may even decide to use your skills to solve some of life's mysteries.

9 MONDAY *Moon Age Day 28 Moon Sign Leo*

You are capable of achieving a high professional profile this week and of making sure that people take notice of your opinions. That is why it is so important to put your ideas forward and to convince others to follow your lead. Concentration should come easily under present trends, and personal successes can be the result.

10 TUESDAY *Moon Age Day 0 Moon Sign Leo*

Trends support a slight sensitivity to criticism right now, and you may well decide to withdraw from certain issues if you suspect that not everyone is on your side. These are more likely to be personal than professional situations, though it's worth asking yourself whether you are reacting too harshly to nothing tangible. It is important to be optimistic.

11 WEDNESDAY *Moon Age Day 1 Moon Sign Virgo*

This would be a great time to extend yourself in social situations and to make others sit up and take notice of your all-round personality. When it comes to solving problems you can be second to none, and you shouldn't have any difficulty breaking new ground or acquiring skills you didn't have before.

12 THURSDAY *Moon Age Day 2 Moon Sign Virgo*

You needn't allow your present desire for peace and harmony to stifle your creative instincts or prevent you from speaking out if you feel strongly about a particular issue. It would also be quite easy today to allow others to take advantage of your good nature, and this is something you should guard against in almost any situation.

13 FRIDAY *Moon Age Day 3 Moon Sign Libra*

There could be just a hint of irrationality whilst the Moon occupies your solar twelfth house, and it would be easy to mistake this for intuition. The two things are quite different, as you will soon learn if you follow instincts led by superstition. Your best approach is to keep your mind focused on the real world and leave phantoms to the realms of fiction.

14 SATURDAY *Moon Age Day 4 Moon Sign Libra*

If you are at work today you can make great gains, because most of the positive trends at the moment favour your professional life rather than your personal one. All the same you can afford to enjoy yourself and have fun, especially with good friends, even if there are a few issues to deal with as far as family relationships are concerned.

15 SUNDAY *Moon Age Day 5 Moon Sign Libra*

By tomorrow the lunar high could give you such a jolt into action that you might be surprised at the intensity of it. You would be wise to get any unfinished jobs out of the way today, though this may demand a degree of concentration you find difficult to achieve. Try to avoid letting your mind wander right now.

16 MONDAY *Moon Age Day 6 Moon Sign Scorpio*

You have scope to make this a really excellent start to a new week, with things going your way and falling into place without you really having to try too hard. There is a certain element of luck about, encouraging you to play your hunches without much fear of coming unstuck. Confidence grows regarding an important personal matter.

17 TUESDAY *Moon Age Day 7 Moon Sign Scorpio*

What really matters today is the way you can get others on your side, which will prove to be of great important if you want to try something new and revolutionary. Achieving any sort of goal ought to be easier with the lunar high around, and you can even persuade people who usually behave in an awkward manner to be more helpful.

18 WEDNESDAY *Moon Age Day 8 Moon Sign Sagittarius*

Venus is now in your solar twelfth house, supporting an interlude when you may be quite sensitive and impressionable. This is fine when it comes to understanding the motivations of those around you, but too much sensitivity can also lead you to lose confidence or to feel that the world is not on your side. At all costs avoid a persecution complex!

19 THURSDAY *Moon Age Day 9 Moon Sign Sagittarius*

Not only is Venus in your solar twelfth house but the planet Mars is there too. This indicates a degree of impracticality, even regarding tasks you have undertaken many times before. You can best avoid tensions building up in personal attachments by telling it how it is. At the same time, listening carefully to what others have to say can work wonders.

20 FRIDAY *Moon Age Day 10 Moon Sign Capricorn*

Do you feel restless and impatient to do something quite different? Most of your planetary positions at the moment will cry out for you to make changes, which are also good because they can help you to take your mind off issues that are not half as difficult as they seem at the moment. The busier you are, the happier you can become.

21 SATURDAY ☿ *Moon Age Day 11 Moon Sign Capricorn*

Your professional life can now benefit from a degree of good fortune, though it may be difficult to register this fact at the weekend. If you do work today, you should make the most of opportunities to speak to those who are higher up the tree than you are, and in any situation you should not be afraid to speak out if you know a plan of action is brilliant.

22 SUNDAY ☿ *Moon Age Day 12 Moon Sign Capricorn*

Emotions could now be very close to the surface, especially when you are at home. And bear in mind that you are not the only person who can fire off without thinking. This could lead to unnecessary misunderstandings and even arguments. Scorpio doesn't argue very often, but there's a danger of vitriol when you do get in gear.

23 MONDAY ☿ *Moon Age Day 13 Moon Sign Aquarius*

You have scope to achieve a good start to the new week. Your consideration for others is emphasised, in fact in some ways probably too much so, but you do have the ability to take life in your stride to a much greater extent than you have been doing recently. The time is right to get involved in new projects, especially ones with a social angle.

24 TUESDAY ☿ *Moon Age Day 14 Moon Sign Aquarius*

In friendship issues you can now draw people together, which also means being able to get them to follow your lead. It's worth getting onside with those who seem to have a good understanding of what is needed, especially at work. You can also use this interlude to ease the problems of anyone who is going through a really hard time right now.

25 WEDNESDAY ☿ *Moon Age Day 15 Moon Sign Pisces*

The spotlight is on the helpful side of your nature, and especially so whilst Venus stays in your solar twelfth house. Your strength lies in your willingness to be of service to others, and in your ability to find very practical ways to be of assistance. Don't worry about the end of jobs, but simply concentrate in a minute-by-minute sense.

26 THURSDAY ☿ *Moon Age Day 16 Moon Sign Pisces*

Beware of being led up the garden path by false promises. It pays to keep your eyes out for duplicitous people around now and to avoid them at all cost. Your intuition should be your best guide at present and it is unlikely to let you down. In romantic terms you can now be more powerful and dominant than you think.

27 FRIDAY ☿ *Moon Age Day 17 Moon Sign Pisces*

Even if you are now working hard and very conscientiously, it might be difficult to become as integrated into groups or organisations as you would wish. You need to ask yourself whether the failure is actually yours, or whether you are the victim of disagreements that have nothing to do with you. What you require now is a very philosophical attitude.

28 SATURDAY ☿ *Moon Age Day 18 Moon Sign Aries*

This has potential to be one of the better days of the month as far as social pleasures are concerned. It's natural to turn your mind this way and that to try to make sense of all that is taking place around you, but a more settled approach is now possible, and could be the route to contentment. An ideal day to spend time with family members.

29 SUNDAY ☿ *Moon Age Day 19 Moon Sign Aries*

You needn't allow others to influence your attitude or actions when you know that your own opinions are worth following. Rather than capitulating, it pays to talk sensibly until you can bring people round to your point of view. Scorpio is often inclined to take the lead, even if it is also sometime lacking in overall confidence or self-belief.

30 MONDAY ☿ *Moon Age Day 20 Moon Sign Taurus*

If energy levels seem lower for the next couple of days, your best response would be to concentrate on one job at once. Taking on too much could lead to fatigue and might mean doing nothing properly. There is much to be said for being well ahead of yourself where it really counts, and this should help you to coast along for a while.

31 TUESDAY ☿ *Moon Age Day 21 Moon Sign Taurus*

Obstacles may well be thrown in your path, either by people or by circumstances. What you would be wise to hang on to at this time is your sense of humour, which can be of great use to you whilst the lunar low remains. The more you make jokes and see the funny side of life, the greater the chance that you can make progress.

September
2010

1 WEDNESDAY ☿ *Moon Age Day 22 Moon Sign Gemini*

An underlying theme of renewal now prevails. There are certain facts and issues in your life that need a general reappraisal, and that is what you can bring to bear at the moment. The start of a new month also assists you to gain a better financial understanding, and would be an ideal time to renew a promise that has great personal implications.

2 THURSDAY ☿ *Moon Age Day 23 Moon Sign Gemini*

Relationships with friends are now well starred, and you should have plenty of chance to show just how loyal and caring you are capable of being. There are positive trends associated with working for the sake of other people, though of course there is nothing too surprising about this for Scorpio. Be prepared for people to show their appreciation.

3 FRIDAY ☿ *Moon Age Day 24 Moon Sign Cancer*

More personal freedom becomes possible, and your determination to have your own way is emphasised, especially where the organisation of your life is concerned. You needn't be anyone's pawn under present trends, and if you feel you are being put upon in any way you can afford to dig in your heels. A day to welcome new characters into your life.

4 SATURDAY ☿ *Moon Age Day 25 Moon Sign Cancer*

There is a slight sense of detachment whilst Venus occupies its present position, and that could mean that personal relationships don't have quite the intensity that you and maybe other people would wish. It isn't that you fail to care, but showing exactly how deep your emotions run may not be too easy at the present time.

5 SUNDAY ☿ *Moon Age Day 26 Moon Sign Leo*

Life itself has the ability to help you into the spotlight on this particular Sunday, and it's worth seeking opportunities to take centre stage in social matters. Your organisational skills count for a great deal now, and you can use them at home to make you feel more comfortable and to prepare for the beautiful autumn months.

6 MONDAY ☿ *Moon Age Day 27 Moon Sign Leo*

Friendship issues should be positively highlighted today, assisting you to bring a touch of magic and warmth to both old and new encounters. If people are pleased to have you close to them, you may be able to persuade them to divulge their most intimate secrets. You can afford to take up a positive and generally optimistic frame of mind.

7 TUESDAY ☿ *Moon Age Day 28 Moon Sign Leo*

You are better off today if you can put yourself amongst groups of people or in situations where sharing becomes a possibility. Going it alone is not to be recommended for the moment, and the focus is on what you can do to support and encourage people who may not have been having a good time recently.

8 WEDNESDAY ☿ *Moon Age Day 0 Moon Sign Virgo*

Your influence over life is quite noteworthy today. There are gains to be made on the financial front, though the most important steps you take might have little or nothing to do with money. You can afford to make love a strong factor in your thinking and decision-making, and should have what it takes to increase your personal popularity across the board.

9 THURSDAY ☿ *Moon Age Day 1 Moon Sign Virgo*

Your strength lies in your ability to draw on your previous experiences and bring what you have learned to whatever situation is surrounding you at the moment. Rather than being tied to rules and regulations under present trends, your best approach is to be ready to do things in your own original way.

10 FRIDAY ☿ *Moon Age Day 2 Moon Sign Libra*

The Moon now encourages a very idealistic frame of mind, and you can use this to identify exactly what it is you want. Nevertheless, there is still an emphasis on your concern for other people. There are signs that almost everything you do today has an ulterior motive, but nearly everything also has an altruistic twist.

11 SATURDAY ☿ *Moon Age Day 3 Moon Sign Libra*

Even if you can't get to where you want to be quite as quickly as you would wish, the Moon in your solar twelfth house supports a thoughtful approach and assists you to make progress of a steady but certain sort. Today is about seeking out the love and concern of others, and making the most of the warmth you can attract, especially in terms of romance.

12 SUNDAY ☿ *Moon Age Day 4 Moon Sign Scorpio*

You now have exactly what it takes to get the sort of results you are looking for. There is everything to play for whilst the lunar high predominates, and since it continues into a new working week, you can use at least part of today to get yourself ready for the flurry of activity that you should be directing towards your career tomorrow.

13 MONDAY ☿ *Moon Age Day 5 Moon Sign Scorpio*

Your spirits are lifted no end, and you have scope to positively fly towards your objectives on a day that offers so much in terms of energy and enthusiasm. Today is an excellent opportunity to get people who matter the most on your side. It's time to play your natural good luck for all it is worth.

14 TUESDAY *Moon Age Day 6 Moon Sign Sagittarius*

This has potential to be a period of great significance to romantically inclined Scorpios. Venus is now in your solar first house, bringing the possibility of sudden and sometimes completely unexpected flashes of attraction. The responses you can gain from others can also be surprising in a non-romantic sense. Why not call in a few favours now?

15 WEDNESDAY *Moon Age Day 7 Moon Sign Sagittarius*

Finances are well starred at this stage of the week. Perhaps you can obtain money from unexpected directions, or you may be paid back fully in terms of a loan you made. This would be a good day to sign contracts or to take on new financial deals, particularly if you are willing to read the small print very carefully.

16 THURSDAY *Moon Age Day 8 Moon Sign Capricorn*

Communication issues could now bring a few disappointments. This is not a strong trend and it shouldn't last long, but for today at least it may be difficult to make yourself understood, or, worse still, to get others to listen at all. Your ability to sort out awkward situations could well come in very handy at present.

17 FRIDAY *Moon Age Day 9 Moon Sign Capricorn*

Even if you can't avoid challenges today, with Mars now in your solar first house that shouldn't really matter because you have what it takes to deal with them quite easily. The strength of your own capabilities can help you to turn a few heads in both professional and social settings. Be disciplined when you know that something is really important.

18 SATURDAY *Moon Age Day 10 Moon Sign Capricorn*

A preoccupation with the past is a legacy of current trends, and when Scorpio starts looking back it can have a great bearing on the present. You needn't assume that because something turned out in a particular way before it will do so again now. It's important to keep your mind focused on what is around the next corner, and to welcome it.

19 SUNDAY *Moon Age Day 11 Moon Sign Aquarius*

Impatience is symptomatic of this period, and you may not be too keen to go through the same old rigmarole time and again. People who constantly delay things won't impress you, and being punctual is the name of the game for you. You don't mind rules and regulations at the moment, just as long as you are making them up!

20 MONDAY *Moon Age Day 12 Moon Sign Aquarius*

You can use your charms to attract a generally warm response when it comes to social encounters and matters associated with romance. There could be attention coming your way from a more or less unexpected direction, and your best approach is to be quite definite in your affections. You may even learn to like someone you once hated.

21 TUESDAY *Moon Age Day 13 Moon Sign Pisces*

Beware of rushing into important decisions. It would be better by far to delay making up your mind than to do something that will turn out to be unwise or even downright foolish. There are good reasons to seek advice from those you trust at this time, and to check out all relevant details before committing yourself to any arrangements.

22 WEDNESDAY *Moon Age Day 14 Moon Sign Pisces*

Relationships can be given a boost under present planetary trends. You have what it takes to make this one of the most romantic interludes of the year, and to make the most of the wonderful compliments you can attract. This may not be enough to prevent a touch of temper on your part if others are determined to do stupid things.

23 THURSDAY *Moon Age Day 15 Moon Sign Pisces*

Even if you manage to get professional matters working out as you would wish, you might have to be more attentive when it comes to social invitations or offers of group activities. There is just a slight chance you will get yourself involved in something that turns out to be far more trouble that it is worth. Be prepared to listen to good advice today.

24 FRIDAY *Moon Age Day 16 Moon Sign Aries*

Today works best if you are willing to labour industriously behind the scenes in order to get things exactly right in your life as a whole. Even if you aren't quite as 'up front' as you have been, but that doesn't mean you can't get involved. Sometimes it is the quiet side of Scorpio that gets the most done, and it's time that people recognised the fact.

25 SATURDAY *Moon Age Day 17 Moon Sign Aries*

An ideal day to ensure your love life is eventful and enjoyable. Scorpio people who are involved in deep attachments should be able to get the heat rising, and those of you who are looking for a new attachment should keep your eyes open today. Sometimes romance can spring up from the most surprising and least likely directions.

26 SUNDAY *Moon Age Day 18 Moon Sign Taurus*

This could turn out to be quite a dull day, but it really depends on the amount of effort you are willing to put in. Ask yourself whether it's worth going to too much trouble, because during the lunar low even if you move mountains you might find nothing of interest under them. Simply accept what life offers you and keep your eyes open for later.

27 MONDAY *Moon Age Day 19 Moon Sign Taurus*

There could be challenges to your confidence arising around this time. If others don't appear to have too much faith in your abilities, you need to consider whether some of the problem exists in your mind rather than in reality. Let others do some of the hard work today. The responsibility will do them good and the break from duty will benefit you.

28 TUESDAY *Moon Age Day 20 Moon Sign Taurus*

You may find you are unable to cope if you take on too many responsibilities at this time. This is not to suggest that you are failing to do what is necessary to keep forward motion going in your life. It's really just a case of choosing your activities carefully and leaving some of the major tasks until another more positive day.

29 WEDNESDAY *Moon Age Day 21 Moon Sign Gemini*

Putting your creative talents to good use is not the same as being selfish. In any case if you profit from life at this time you can afford to make sure that others benefit too. There is much to be said for developing an individualistic and highly original style of working. Even if others don't understand it, you can succeed on your own terms.

30 THURSDAY *Moon Age Day 22 Moon Sign Gemini*

Venus remains in your solar first house and can offer assistance when it comes to promoting your own self-image. You needn't be stuck for an idea today, and you have what it takes to make others sit up and take notice. Remember that anniversaries and birthdays are important, especially those within your family.

October

2010

1 FRIDAY *Moon Age Day 23 Moon Sign Cancer*

Mars in its present position suggests that you could be confronted by the odd issue that will prove difficult to sort out. It can also support a bad-tempered approach on occasions, particularly if you are sorely tried by others. Be prepared to deal patiently with any mechanical problems.

2 SATURDAY *Moon Age Day 24 Moon Sign Cancer*

Try to broaden your horizons as much as proves to be possible this weekend and make the most of any remaining good weather in order to get out of the house. You need to do things that you find stimulating and interesting, rather than sticking to mundane domestic chores that would only serve to make you feel frustrated.

3 SUNDAY *Moon Age Day 25 Moon Sign Leo*

In some ways you could now find yourself at an important crossroads. Even if this has to do with your career and is not strictly relevant at the weekend, you have a chance to get your mind working hard to find the solutions you require. One option is to seek advice from family members or your partner.

4 MONDAY *Moon Age Day 26 Moon Sign Leo*

Beware of relying entirely on your intuition when it comes to important matters. As a rule your almost psychic nature is your best guide, though this may not be the case around now. It is facts and figures that really count, together with the tried and tested advice of people who have done the same thing you are facing now time and again.

5 TUESDAY *Moon Age Day 27 Moon Sign Virgo*

Most relationships should be favourably highlighted and you can really exert a positive influence on life while Venus remains in your solar first house. Now is the time to show others how charming, inspirational and charismatic you can be. Difficulties are now possible with Earth-sign individuals such as those born under Taurus or Virgo.

6 WEDNESDAY *Moon Age Day 28 Moon Sign Virgo*

Yet another boost to teamwork and group activities is on offer today, courtesy of the rapidly moving Moon. In any situation it is important not to argue for your limitations at the moment, but rather to have more confidence in your ability to learn as you go along. Experience is a fine thing, but it has to come from doing a job.

7 THURSDAY *Moon Age Day 29 Moon Sign Libra*

Trends suggest you could be your own worst critic today, which is something of a shame at a time when things could be going very well for you. If you do lack patience with yourself you might not do as well as you would if you remained optimistic regarding the outcome of any situation. A day to keep abreast of local news and views.

8 FRIDAY *Moon Age Day 0 Moon Sign Libra*

Are you coming under pressure to rethink your strategies, particularly at work? It's fine to look again at certain issues, though there is much to be said for sticking to your own guns with things as they are in a planetary sense. Of course you need to show yourself willing to listen to another point of view, but in the end it is your opinions that really count.

9 SATURDAY *Moon Age Day 1 Moon Sign Scorpio*

Today is about calling the shots, and the lunar high brings the best possible potential for you to create a weekend of fun and happy encounters. You needn't keep busy all the time, because your social inclinations are also important, and you need to have fun! Break out and get well away from the usual concerns of a domestic Saturday.

10 SUNDAY *Moon Age Day 2 Moon Sign Scorpio*

You should be tapping into all your available energy, and you shouldn't be tardy when it comes to getting involved in anything that stretches your abilities and offers excitement. This is an ideal time to improve your financial standing, perhaps by seeking to raise money in ways you never quite thought of previously.

11 MONDAY *Moon Age Day 3 Moon Sign Sagittarius*

A few practical mishaps are possible today, particularly if you are too inclined to rush things. Your best approach is to try to settle to what you are doing and make sure you do things one at once. You have what it takes to attract a great deal of attention from people who are especially fond of you and to gain practical help if you need it.

12 TUESDAY *Moon Age Day 4 Moon Sign Sagittarius*

Whether you would rather keep a low profile today or not, you have the ability to dominate your surroundings, supported by that first-house Mars. Being out there in front is a natural aspect of life now, as is getting others to recognise your leadership potential. Confrontations are best avoided, especially when you are amongst family members.

13 WEDNESDAY *Moon Age Day 5 Moon Sign Sagittarius*

When it comes to your social life you can ensure this is a happy and eventful period. Any sort of dialogue between yourself and others can provide you with new ideas and a renewed sense of purpose regarding practical issues. This would also be a favourable time to try to create comfortable surroundings at home.

14 THURSDAY *Moon Age Day 6 Moon Sign Capricorn*

All communication matters are highlighted by the present position of the Moon, though some of the contacts you make with others may be transitory and perhaps less satisfying than you may have hoped. You can't get on perfectly with everyone, and it might be best to concentrate on those individuals you already know and trust.

15 FRIDAY *Moon Age Day 7 Moon Sign Capricorn*

Home and family are vital issues for you at the best of times, but they seem to be more important than ever as the Moon moves on in your chart later today. Be prepared to enter a new phase in terms of personal attachments, and to give help and advice to anyone, but particularly younger family members.

16 SATURDAY *Moon Age Day 8 Moon Sign Aquarius*

Monotonous work probably won't suit you too well at present, and once again the culprit is the first-house Mars in your solar chart. There is a drive for you to get involved in things you find fascinating and to dominate certain issues if you want to get them out of the way quickly. Your natural sensitivity may be slightly obscured today!

17 SUNDAY *Moon Age Day 9 Moon Sign Aquarius*

Venus is now in your own sign of Scorpio, which is a promising planetary position and good news as far as personal relationships are concerned. It becomes possible for you to show the best side of your nature when it comes to romance, and finding the right compliments to make others feel very special shouldn't be difficult for you.

18 MONDAY *Moon Age Day 10 Moon Sign Aquarius*

There are signs that you might need to change your mind about something major now. Be prepared to respond to any unusual situations and odd coincidences that you experience today. Rather than being spooked by these happenings, your best approach is to treat them as signposts towards a better and more progressive future.

19 TUESDAY *Moon Age Day 11 Moon Sign Pisces*

You have what it takes to remain dynamic and enthusiastic. Not only do you have all the vitality and power you could require, you can also make use of masses of charm and your winning personality, which nobody could ignore. This really can be a major-league time for you and should be treated as one of the best phases of the year in an all-round sense.

20 WEDNESDAY *Moon Age Day 12 Moon Sign Pisces*

Romantically and personally you can take advantage of a winning streak, and if you recognise the intensity of positive situations you can ensure you don't miss out on any of the benefits that are available. By all means stand up for friends in disputes, but wherever possible talk your way out of awkward situations.

21 THURSDAY *Moon Age Day 13 Moon Sign Aries*

Trends suggest you may find it difficult to please your partner for the next couple of days, and what might make matters worse is that the Sun is still in your solar twelfth house – just. This supports a slight lack of tact, and an interlude in which you may not have quite the level of confidence in your own abilities and opinions as you often do.

22 FRIDAY *Moon Age Day 14 Moon Sign Aries*

There are planets around you now that emphasise very strongly your sense of obligation to other people. In some ways this can prove to be quite tiresome, especially if you want to push ahead and think of yourself for once. It isn't selfish to seek personal success, and you can still be as responsible as ever.

23 SATURDAY *Moon Age Day 15 Moon Sign Aries*

Be prepared to deal with obstacles that may be thrown in your path. Before today is too old the approaching lunar low could be making its presence felt. This isn't an ideal time to be travelling long distances, and if you push yourself too hard in a physical sense you could soon tire. In reality this is a favourable time to take a well-earned rest.

24 SUNDAY *Moon Age Day 16 Moon Sign Taurus*

A brief period of inactivity would be no bad thing on the otherwise presently smooth road that is your life. You can afford to let the traffic flow on for a while as you stand and watch contentedly. Frustration is possible if you try to do too much, at a time when the prevailing planetary influences are encouraging you to preserve your energy.

25 MONDAY *Moon Age Day 17 Moon Sign Taurus*

Although it might not seem to be the case as the day gets started, you can now ensure that most of your efforts have success written all over them. A break from everyday routines is still recommended, but not so that you can continue to watch and wait. On the contrary, today is about doing different and stimulating things, perhaps alongside your friends.

26 TUESDAY *Moon Age Day 18 Moon Sign Gemini*

Now you have scope to get things really moving. In addition to Venus and Mars, the Sun has now entered your solar first house, assisting you to make this the happiest and most successful period you can imagine. Of course it's still up to you because fortune is most inclined to favour the bold. Don't wait to be asked – just be progressive!

27 WEDNESDAY *Moon Age Day 19 Moon Sign Gemini*

Partnerships are now favourably highlighted and co-operation becomes the unequivocal key to success. Out here in the middle of the week you can be quite satisfied with your efforts and you seem to have what it takes to be especially popular when you are in good company. A day to get on with jobs you find interesting and stimulating.

28 THURSDAY *Moon Age Day 20 Moon Sign Cancer*

Communication is particularly important now that little Mercury joins all those other planets in your solar first house. What a busy Scorpio you can be, and how well you make the most of chances to get on with people generally. Even if certain of your actions could be seen as somewhat eccentric, ask yourself whether there is anything wrong with that.

29 FRIDAY *Moon Age Day 21 Moon Sign Cancer*

Getting down to brass tacks as far as money is concerned is the order of the day, and trends assist you to order your finances in a very positive sort of way. This is also a time during which you can afford to indulge yourself more than you normally would, and you might even be able to persuade other people to show you their generosity.

30 SATURDAY *Moon Age Day 22 Moon Sign Cancer*

It pays to be out in front and to remain highly personable at the moment. The positive impact you make on the world should be there for all to see. As a result you can get people to take notice of you, which makes this an ideal time for putting your ideas across and for garnering the sort of support you need. Innovations become the norm at present.

31 SUNDAY *Moon Age Day 23 Moon Sign Leo*

There are positive trends associated with getting involved in an interesting social environment, and as a result you might not be trying too hard to get much done in a practical sense today. Your judgement is sound, and you should be able to get onside with the sort of people who get things done. You may even decide to follow their lead later.

November 2010

1 MONDAY *Moon Age Day 24 Moon Sign Leo*

There are now gains to be made by taking a hands-on role when it comes to creating your own future. Scorpio sometimes feels itself locked up in the needs and opinions of other people, but you can take steps to avoid this during the first half of November. A new month offers new perspectives, and the necessary energy to get things moving.

2 TUESDAY *Moon Age Day 25 Moon Sign Virgo*

It's time to take notice of all the interesting things that are taking place around you now. Inspiration becomes important, and you have what it takes to push yourself forward to such an extent that the world and his dog should notice your presence. Don't just prime situations – get on and see them through to completion.

3 WEDNESDAY *Moon Age Day 26 Moon Sign Virgo*

Mars has now moved into your solar second house, and if this planetary position carries any slightly adverse implications for you it could be that it stimulates your more extravagant inclinations. This may not simply be a matter of splashing out more than you normally would financially, because it can also highlight the showy side of your nature.

4 THURSDAY *Moon Age Day 27 Moon Sign Libra*

With the Moon now moving into your solar twelfth house you have a chance to retreat somewhat into your shell, and you may well decide not to be quite as progressive or chatty for the next couple of days as you have recently been. Bear in mind that this might come as a surprise to those who are close to you, so be prepared to reassure them.

5 FRIDAY *Moon Age Day 28 Moon Sign Libra*

There is nothing at all wrong with taking life steadily for a few hours. After all, if you have been running at full speed for a few weeks now you can look back across time and see how much you have managed to achieve and how far you have come. This is only possible when you take time out to relax and contemplate.

6 SATURDAY *Moon Age Day 0 Moon Sign Scorpio*

The lunar high would be an excellent time to break through barriers that may have stood before you for months or even years. Having done so, you can move into new pastures altogether and can achieve some of the successes that might have eluded you for a while. There is much to be said for contacting someone you haven't seen for ages.

7 SUNDAY *Moon Age Day 1 Moon Sign Scorpio*

Communication remains the important component of your life, not just because of the lunar high but also on account of that first-house Mercury. Remember that if you remain quiet, nobody will know what you want, and since your charms are highlighted at the moment you should be able to persuade others to help you further your own plans.

8 MONDAY *Moon Age Day 2 Moon Sign Sagittarius*

More than ever the focus today is on practical ideas and with getting things done as efficiently as possible. You might have to put one or two personal plans on hold, particularly if you can't do everything at the same time, no matter how much you try. Be prepared to pace yourself and get as much fun as possible from the day.

9 TUESDAY *Moon Age Day 3 Moon Sign Sagittarius*

You should now be able to take greater control over your life and its circumstances. This is part of the legacy of the first-house Sun you are experiencing at the moment, and it gives you the opportunity to make this an eventful and generally exciting period. Others may be gearing up for winter, but you can be as lively as a cricket.

10 WEDNESDAY *Moon Age Day 4 Moon Sign Capricorn*

Today is about your ability to deal with harsh words if they occur, possibly between yourself and your life partner. You would be wise to start by finding out what is causing the irritation, and that could mean taking time out from a busy schedule to ask a few questions. Remember that misunderstandings are best dealt with straight away.

11 THURSDAY *Moon Age Day 5 Moon Sign Capricorn*

Your powers are well accented, and you should be keeping your wits about you under most circumstances now. You can afford to be of tremendous help to your friends and even to people you barely know at all. It's a question of using your powers of discrimination to the full and being willing to pass on your acquired wisdom to virtually anyone.

12 FRIDAY *Moon Age Day 6 Moon Sign Capricorn*

The Moon now in your solar fourth house is favourable for all aspects of your home life and for harmonious relationships within the family. By all means decide that the time is right to make certain alterations to your personal surroundings, though it's worth making certain that those you live with are as happy about this as you are!

13 SATURDAY *Moon Age Day 7 Moon Sign Aquarius*

The influence you have over certain people is now less certain than it appeared to be even a few days ago. Before you start anything new, especially if it means relying on others, do make sure that you can gain the co-operation you need. Slight embarrassment could be the result of taking people for granted today.

14 SUNDAY *Moon Age Day 8 Moon Sign Aquarius*

It's all very well seeking personal enjoyment and excitement at present, but going overboard is not to be recommended. You would benefit from a lighter approach and from allowing others to make some of the decisions. Leading from the front can work in some situations, though there is much to be said for being second in command just now.

15 MONDAY *Moon Age Day 9 Moon Sign Pisces*

It might be best not to expect too much from others at this time. When it comes to getting things done you would be wise to consider going it alone, and some relationships could be fraught with complications. In the main you should still be able to make progress, and despite minor frustrations you can win through in most important situations.

16 TUESDAY *Moon Age Day 10 Moon Sign Pisces*

Whilst the Sun remains in its present position it would be sensible to keep thinking big. Start new projects with the expectation of success and that is what you can achieve. This would be an ideal time to welcome new personalities into your life and to make the most of their alternative ways of looking at life and the new opportunities they bring.

17 WEDNESDAY *Moon Age Day 11 Moon Sign Aries*

You can now use your good business mind to make decisions that are shot through with perception and wisdom. It's important to avoid confrontations at work by finding ways to agree with others, yet at the same time managing to get your own way. A little psychology can go a long way right now, and it's something you are good at.

18 THURSDAY *Moon Age Day 12 Moon Sign Aries*

You have scope to remain busy and generally dynamic, and there may not be too many hours available in which to show those closest to you how important they are. But it won't take hours to say 'I love you' or 'you are important to my life'. It's about remembering those who help you on a daily basis and finding little ways to show your gratitude.

19 FRIDAY *Moon Age Day 13 Moon Sign Aries*

There's a risk that fortune could drain away like water through your fingers during today and across the weekend, which is why it is most important to hang on to what you have, particularly in financial terms. The approaching lunar low is a potentially slower time in which certain decisions may be harder. Why not rely on the timely advice of a friend?

20 SATURDAY *Moon Age Day 14 Moon Sign Taurus*

The lunar low is underpinned this month by topsy-turvy influences, some of which could come like a bolt from the blue and knock your reasoning sideways. Your best response is to try alternative points of view and examine situations carefully before you take any sort of action. If it were possible to stand still altogether, now is the time to do it!

21 SUNDAY *Moon Age Day 15 Moon Sign Taurus*

The go-getting side of your nature remains to the fore, even if you find it difficult to go and get precisely what you want for today at least. By tomorrow you should be able to get things more or less back to normal, although the Sun is moving out of your solar first house and into the somewhat more solid second, bringing another change of influence.

22 MONDAY *Moon Age Day 16 Moon Sign Gemini*

Life has held the potential for excitement across the last few weeks, but that could abate now that the Sun is moving on. However, it will be replaced by a greater ability on your part to look to your material needs. A slightly quieter Scorpio could be the result, but you should at least know exactly what you want and how to go about getting it.

23 TUESDAY *Moon Age Day 17 Moon Sign Gemini*

At work you can achieve steady and smooth progress, together with a generally peaceful time at home. This may not be the most exciting period of the year, but you can ensure it is solid and dependable. If there is one thing Scorpio respects it is the ability to know what is coming, and you also like others to be as reliable as you are!

24 WEDNESDAY *Moon Age Day 18 Moon Sign Gemini*

Make the most of a high point of the month as far as travel is concerned. This would be an ideal time to pack your bags and fly off somewhere. Even if this isn't possible in your case, there is much to be said for spreading your wings in some way. Scorpio has a great imagination, and even travelling inside your head would be better than nothing at all.

25 THURSDAY *Moon Age Day 19 Moon Sign Cancer*

Working to realistic deadlines is the order of the day, and is supported by the Sun in Sagittarius. It looks as though fortune will favour some of your recent endeavours, even if your objectives are now slightly more realistic than they were. Stand to make the very best of unexpected comments you are now able to attract.

26 FRIDAY *Moon Age Day 20 Moon Sign Cancer*

The focus is now much more likely to be on your public persona. You needn't hide your light under any sort of bushel, though neither should you be brash or too outspoken. The combination of charisma, charm and practical common sense that you can display now and across the weekend should help you to improve your popularity.

27 SATURDAY *Moon Age Day 21 Moon Sign Leo*

Current trends encourage you to put money and its acquisition firmly at the front of your mind. This doesn't mean you have to avoid the social opportunities that may be available, and if ever there was a good period for mixing business with pleasure, this is it. You can afford to rely on the discretion and promises of those close to you.

28 SUNDAY *Moon Age Day 22 Moon Sign Leo*

In the middle of a phase when the spotlight is on enhanced social activity, you ought to find plenty of opportunities for light relief and for a break from more serious matters. In many situations the current trends assist you to find the answers you need immediately, without having to spend endless hours mulling things over.

29 MONDAY *Moon Age Day 23 Moon Sign Virgo*

A heart-to-heart with your partner or a close relative could help you to uncover hidden issues. There are good reasons to get everything out into the open, because you can't deal with things you can't see. Your strength lies in your ability to bring a greater understanding all round and to dispel misunderstandings. This is a good time to clear the air.

30 TUESDAY *Moon Age Day 24 Moon Sign Virgo*

Monetary matters are brought into sharp focus with the Sun in your solar second house, and there are gains to be made through concentrating on financial issues and working to bring greater security into your life. In particular this is an ideal interlude for looking at the future and storing up acorns ahead of a period that could be less certain.

December

2010

1 WEDNESDAY *Moon Age Day 25 Moon Sign Libra*

Now is the time the make the very most of the positive romantic trends that surround you. Venus did a little detour back into your solar twelfth house but now it is back in your first house again. This is favourable for all personal attachments and it also assists you to be more specific in the way you speak those all-important words of love.

2 THURSDAY *Moon Age Day 26 Moon Sign Libra*

This may be the best time of all to confide your feelings to loved ones and to get on with sorting things out as far as your home is concerned. Be as sympathetic as you can to anyone who is presently having difficulties, and show just how helpful the sign of Scorpio can be. If pointless routines bore you, why not avoid them today?

3 FRIDAY *Moon Age Day 27 Moon Sign Scorpio*

The lunar high arrives, and you can now afford to back your hunches and to take chances you might normally avoid. You can use your forceful and dynamic nature to make sure others notice that you are around, and you should also be displaying significant charm in social settings. This is definitely a wonderful day to be out and about.

4 SATURDAY *Moon Age Day 28 Moon Sign Scorpio*

New avenues open up for you as far as your personal dreams and schemes are concerned. It's time to take advantage of a winning streak and to do what you can to bring good things to those you love. Be prepared to make this a weekend of fun and to show how childlike you can be in your approach, no matter what your age.

5 SUNDAY *Moon Age Day 29 Moon Sign Sagittarius*

Practical affairs are well accented. Now is a favourable time for consolidation and for finding the time you need to let others know the way your mind is working on many different levels. Simply sitting around and talking can be very important, and gives you the opportunity to catch up on all sorts of news you didn't know before.

6 MONDAY *Moon Age Day 0 Moon Sign Sagittarius*

This would be an ideal time to look again at money and to decide how best you can use your resources more wisely. There's nothing wrong with being inventive when it comes to Christmas gifts and refusing to squander cash on non-essentials. With the present position of the Sun you have scope to tap into some useful and quite innovative ideas.

7 TUESDAY *Moon Age Day 1 Moon Sign Capricorn*

A communicative approach is the name of the game today and you have everything you need to achieve little changes at work that can make all the difference in the longer term. Not everyone is going to be on your side, either professionally or socially, but when the chips are down you should be able to find people you can rely on.

8 WEDNESDAY *Moon Age Day 2 Moon Sign Capricorn*

Everything seems to focus on your love life around now, which is why a little extra effort could prove to be quite useful. Make sure the most important person in your life knows how significant they are to you – which means telling them, of course! This is not the time to be taking those you care about for granted.

9 THURSDAY *Moon Age Day 3 Moon Sign Capricorn*

Trends suggest that some strong nostalgic influences are beginning to gather. It could be the time of year, or maybe the fact that you are more inclined to look back than forward. Whatever the reason, your best response is to make sure you focus plenty of attention now on the present and future. Remember that past events are not always your best guide.

10 FRIDAY *Moon Age Day 4 Moon Sign Aquarius*

Property and financial interests are now positively highlighted in your solar chart. The key is to remain basically innovative and to capitalise on good ideas as to how you can increase your fortune and your influence in the days ahead. If you decide to splash out on anything around now, a gift for your partner could certainly work wonders.

11 SATURDAY ☿ *Moon Age Day 5 Moon Sign Aquarius*

Whilst you might consider that your tendency to speak out and to tell the truth is a positive thing, you need to ask yourself whether others see it that way. There are times when a little sugar on the pill is to be recommended, and you may not get far today if those closest to you find your attitude somewhat brutal. Tact is important, so why not use it?

12 SUNDAY ☿ *Moon Age Day 6 Moon Sign Pisces*

In terms of your personality you could dominate the scenery today, and you may still be inclined to push your ideas forward, even if it is quite obvious that some people do not agree with you. If things begin to go wrong at any level, the last thing you should do is to panic. Simply retrench and start again, slowly and steadily.

13 MONDAY ☿ *Moon Age Day 7 Moon Sign Pisces*

A period of consolidation and security is to be advised, and is the best way of avoiding overspending and maybe losing control of your finances. This can be an expensive time of year but there are ways in which you can keep things to a reasonable level. Better by far to think hard now than to regret your spending later.

14 TUESDAY ☿ *Moon Age Day 8 Moon Sign Pisces*

The quickened pace of life assists you to stay on your toes and to enjoy diverse interests to a greater extent. Rather than looking in just one direction for answers, your best approach is to look in many. Co-operation is also emphasised, and your abilities in this area should help in your efforts to obtain the support you need from others.

15 WEDNESDAY ☿ *Moon Age Day 9 Moon Sign Aries*

Venus in your first house gives you scope to improve your love life – even if you thought it was perfectly fine before. Getting people to take greater notice of you is the first step to attracting many more compliments. Romance is the name of the game and new beginnings are there for the taking for some Scorpios now.

16 THURSDAY ☿ *Moon Age Day 10 Moon Sign Aries*

You can quicken the speed of life even more, and with Mercury in your third house now it's all about communication in one way or another. Even if you make sure today's events are very brisk, they can also be quite educational and you should relish the chance to increase your knowledge across the board. Saying the right thing is a piece of cake now.

17 FRIDAY ☿ *Moon Age Day 11 Moon Sign Taurus*

Be prepared to deal with any mental tension that arises as the lunar low arrives. Such is the speed of your life at the moment that you may almost fail to notice the restrictions that the Moon in Taurus can bring, though by tomorrow you may decide that the brakes really should be applied.

18 SATURDAY ☿ *Moon Age Day 12 Moon Sign Taurus*

Fortunes may be in the doldrums, but that doesn't necessarily mean that major problems will emerge. On the contrary, you can afford to remain generally resilient, even if you have to undertake the same job more than once. You would be wise to keep your money in your purse or wallet for today, and hold back on your spending until next week.

19 SUNDAY ☿ *Moon Age Day 13 Moon Sign Taurus*

With Venus, the planet of love, in your zodiac sign at the moment you have an opportunity to make this a very exciting time in terms of your emotions. There are signs that you could be taken by surprise by the strength of someone's feelings about you. Bear in mind that not all the attention you attract may be welcome.

20 MONDAY ☿ *Moon Age Day 14 Moon Sign Gemini*

This is an ideal time to sort out basic issues ahead of the Christmas period and to decide what your plans are going to be. Overcrowding your schedule is not to be recommended, or else instead of benefiting from the upcoming holiday period you will end up more fatigued. A day to jettison a few redundant ideas and move forward in your thinking.

21 TUESDAY ☿ *Moon Age Day 15 Moon Sign Gemini*

The focus is on your ability to deal with specific issues you face today, and this is a legacy of the present position of Mars in your solar third house. This position of Mars also supports a slightly more outspoken approach, though you need to ensure that this doesn't give way to temper. There are times today when counting to ten would be no bad thing.

22 WEDNESDAY ☿ *Moon Age Day 16 Moon Sign Cancer*

Your independent mental approach and the way you solve problems assist you to increase your popularity, and there's nothing wrong with offering advice to others throughout most of today and on towards the holidays. Your strength lies in your ability to think on your feet, and you can certainly afford to ooze confidence.

23 THURSDAY ☿ *Moon Age Day 17 Moon Sign Cancer*

Ideas are all very well, but if you have too many at the moment it could be difficult to get the majority of them off the ground prior to the Christmas period. You may decide to keep certain issues on hold until the New Year. Although this could be frustrating on one level, on another you can see it as a source of excitement for the future.

24 FRIDAY ☿ *Moon Age Day 18 Moon Sign Leo*

Christmas Eve is a chance for you to move much closer to something you have wanted for ages. This could also be a favourable day for expressing your emotions and for getting onside with your lover. Today's social influences encourage you to welcome new personalities into your life, and you could even make a new friend for life.

25 SATURDAY ☿ *Moon Age Day 19 Moon Sign Leo*

You have what it takes to form new and even more significant friendships across the Christmas period, even if you don't actually move far from your immediate circles as far as today is concerned. There are good reasons to concentrate your efforts right now on making sure that others have a really good time and get on well with each other.

26 SUNDAY ☿ *Moon Age Day 20 Moon Sign Virgo*

Variety can certainly be the spice of life for Boxing Day, and although trends encouraged you to stick around the homestead yesterday, there is less reason for you to do so today. Your powers of persuasion are at a peak, so if there is someone you want to influence you could hardly pick a better time than this to turn on the charm and convince them.

27 MONDAY ☿ *Moon Age Day 21 Moon Sign Virgo*

There are some wonderful responses on offer in terms of your social life, as well as the chance to get others to fall in line with your wishes. You may not have to persuade your lover to follow a particular course of action – they might already be there!

28 TUESDAY ☿ *Moon Age Day 22 Moon Sign Libra*

Be prepared to deal with a few limitations today as far as your own mind is concerned as you enter a short phase of potential uncertainty. Gains can be made as a result of the generosity of those around you, particularly that of family members.

29 WEDNESDAY ☿ *Moon Age Day 23 Moon Sign Libra*

Trend support a more argumentative approach today, so this may not be the best interlude for co-operating or sharing what you have with others. On the contrary, the selfish side of Scorpio is emphasised, though fortunately not for long.

30 THURSDAY ☿ *Moon Age Day 24 Moon Sign Scorpio*

A day to put yourself at the very forefront of anything that is happening around you, particularly if you are the one doing all the organising! You can use the power of the lunar high to get others to follow your lead and to influence life generally.

31 FRIDAY *Moon Age Day 25 Moon Sign Scorpio*

The last day of the year can prove to be one of the best if you make full use of the good fortune available. Looking forward is the key today, because any ideas you lay down now are well accented for the future.

RISING SIGNS FOR SCORPIO

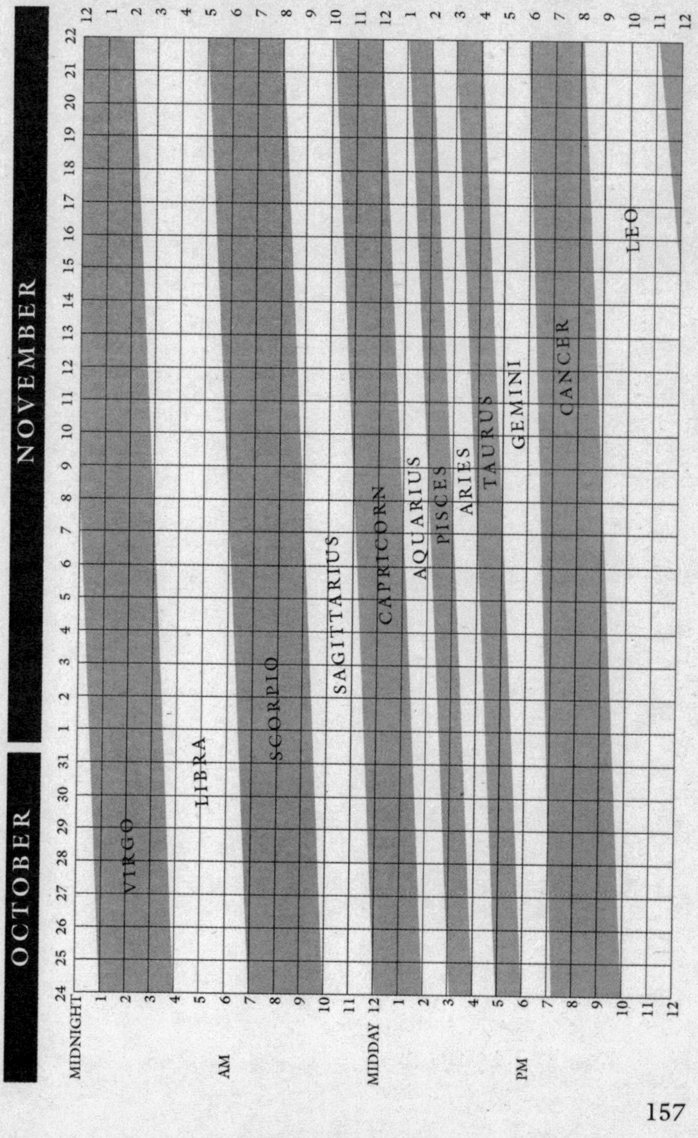

THE ZODIAC, PLANETS AND CORRESPONDENCES

The Earth revolves around the Sun once every calendar year, so when viewed from Earth the Sun appears in a different part of the sky as the year progresses. In astrology, these parts of the sky are divided into the signs of the zodiac and this means that the signs are organised in a circle. The circle begins with Aries and ends with Pisces.

Taking the zodiac sign as a starting point, astrologers then work with all the positions of planets, stars and many other factors to calculate horoscopes and birth charts and tell us what the stars have in store for us.

The table below shows the planets and Elements for each of the signs of the zodiac. Each sign belongs to one of the four Elements: Fire, Air, Earth or Water. Fire signs are creative and enthusiastic; Air signs are mentally active and thoughtful; Earth signs are constructive and practical; Water signs are emotional and have strong feelings.

It also shows the metals and gemstones associated with, or corresponding with, each sign. The correspondence is made when a metal or stone possesses properties that are held in common with a particular sign of the zodiac.

Finally, the table shows the opposite of each star sign – this is the opposite sign in the astrological circle.

Placed	Sign	Symbol	Element	Planet	Metal	Stone	Opposite
1	Aries	Ram	Fire	Mars	Iron	Bloodstone	Libra
2	Taurus	Bull	Earth	Venus	Copper	Sapphire	Scorpio
3	Gemini	Twins	Air	Mercury	Mercury	Tiger's Eye	Sagittarius
4	Cancer	Crab	Water	Moon	Silver	Pearl	Capricorn
5	Leo	Lion	Fire	Sun	Gold	Ruby	Aquarius
6	Virgo	Maiden	Earth	Mercury	Mercury	Sardonyx	Pisces
7	Libra	Scales	Air	Venus	Copper	Sapphire	Aries
8	Scorpio	Scorpion	Water	Pluto	Plutonium	Jasper	Taurus
9	Sagittarius	Archer	Fire	Jupiter	Tin	Topaz	Gemini
10	Capricorn	Goat	Earth	Saturn	Lead	Black Onyx	Cancer
11	Aquarius	Waterbearer	Air	Uranus	Uranium	Amethyst	Leo
12	Pisces	Fishes	Water	Neptune	Tin	Moonstone	Virgo